Kingdom
Commandos

A Training Manual
for God's Elite
Special Forces

by Chip Hill

Published by:
Destiny Image
P.O. Box 351
Shippensburg, PA 17257
717-532-3040

All Scripture Quotations Are From the King James Version (KJV)
or the New American Standard Version (NAS) Unless Otherwise
Noted.

I.S.B.N.-0-914903-16-0

To all Christians, young and old alike, who aspire to greatness in God's Kingdom.

An Elite Army

Moreover, Uzziah had an army ready for battle, which entered into battle by divisions, according to the number of their muster. . . . They were an elite army *. . . who could wage war in great power, to help the king against the enemy.*
Hence his name spread afar, for he was marvelously helped until he was strong. (2 Chron. 26:11,13,15 NAS, emphasis mine)

The Church of Jesus Christ on the Earth
  An elite army—one trained, prepared, and more than ready to enter into the war of the ages. An elite breed of spiritual warriors, ready and able to wage war in great power, to help King Jesus against His enemies. The elite of God, ready to preach the Gospel of the Kingdom to the ends of the earth, making Jesus' name known by all, subduing His enemies by His power, until He returns and the kingdoms on this earth become the kingdoms of our God and then shall the end come.

Contents

This prophecy was given through Chip Hill in Monterey, VA, in July 1985.

People called by the Name of the Lord shall rise up in this hour. Yes, this is the time of God's power and the hour of your going forth into the harvest field. The oppressed and the afflicted have sat quietly waiting for those who would bring them the full gospel message— but no one has come. The people of God have grown fat and dull and are even till now, content to sit in their houses of worship and go to no one. What an abominable thing, says the Lord! That will soon come to an end! For I will require certain men and women of my Word to begin to stir up the army of Jesus Christ, to stir them to bold action, says the Lord; and the army will begin to respond. At first there will be only a few, but as time goes on, more will rise to their feet and blow God's horn of deliverance. I need my army to go forth, to take the battle to the enemy in his trenches and wreak havoc among his troops, declaring the acceptable year of the Lord and setting the captives free! They shall bind and loose, and declare the righteous decrees of the Lord like never before in all of history. My Spirit is pregnant with the signs and wonders you've only dreamed about, yea, miraculous attestations of divine glory await you, saith the Lord! I need a people who will saturate themselves with the four gospels and the book of Acts, a people to remember the former things, and use them as incentive to take hold of my mighty weapons and empty the prison houses of hell on earth! This shall be done, says the Lord, for I said it would and my word shall stand. I will do my pleasure in bringing to the front my word as a witness to all men, and then shall the end come! Not a thing will be taken away from this and men will fear before me!

So stir up yourself my child. Make your calling and election sure. Have done with lesser things and go for the gold! I'm beckoning you, says your God. I call you to be strong and of much courage as you boldly take my Word to your family, neighbors and friends. The hour of the quiet witness is over. I need spokesmen! Spokesmen in the marketplace! Spokesmen on the country lane! Spokesmen to enter into every house to declare the Word of the Lord! And as you go, you will joy in the salvation of the Lord as you see the lost run into the kingdom, the sick healed, and the oppressed go free. Yes, the greatest of opportunities await you, says the Lord. Fling yourself into the midst of what I'm doing! Gladly give your life to something that will last forever! They're doing it in Africa! They're doing it in India! They're doing it all over the world—because I've birthed this thing, says the Lord!

Foreword

The Church of Jesus Christ is entering the most exciting stage of it's history. As we come to the last portion of the 20th Century, the command given to us by our Commander in Chief rings across the ages, "Go into all the world, and preach the good news to all creation . . . and these signs shall follow those who believe, in my name they will cast out demons . . . they shall lay hands on the sick and they shall recover." I believe we are to fulfill that command in our generation.

This will entail a great confrontation with the powers of darkness. We must not shrink back in fear from this conflict. With boldness, under the anointing of the Holy Spirit, we must attack and overpower "the gates of hell."

I remember a fateful night in Zaire, Africa, where I was ministering the good news of Jesus to a crowd of more than 200,000 natives. Most of them were under bondage to witchcraft. Thousands of sorcerers were in the crowd. I ministered mass deliverance and saw literally thousands healed and delivered, with 25,000 decisions for Christ that evening. God had given me a rhema word, which became a mighty weapon against the powers of darkness that night. I declared to the crowd, "One drop of the blood of Jesus destroys the kingdom of Satan!" Evil forces trembled and fled at that declaration.

Chip Hill has written a book you will find helpful in understanding principles that will assist you to confront the powers of darkness, and get the victory for yourself, your family, and for the work of the gospel.

Chip gives us a penetrating look into God's Word, giving us further insight into the principles of spiritual warfare. I appreciate the desire Chip Hill has to serve the Body of Christ, and I commend him and his book to you. May the Lord Jesus Christ be exalted and His kingdom be furthered through the reading of this book.

Mahesh Chavda
Mahesh Chavda Ministries International

Preface

The Church stands poised to execute rescue operations of lightning-fast speed deep into enemy territory. Prisoners-of-war, lost and blinded to the truth, are being held there in dismal captivity. The weak, sick, and demon-oppressed are also there. These prisoners are treated mercilessly by a cruel task-master whose appetite for the suffering of others is gargantuan. These P.O.W.s, whose numbers reach into the billions, sit hopelessly enslaved, and they cry within themselves for some-one to come and lift their heavy burdens, for someone who will set them free.

There are, in this diseased and warped world, many who have yet to hear the gospel message for the first time. Even in America there are those who have not heard the good news. In Charlotte, North Carolina, for example, we once met a young black man from the city's ghetto who had never heard the story of the cross. He didn't know who Jesus was. I realized that he was only one of thousands in his city alone. In many ways, the ghettos of America's major cities are just as enslaving as the hard hand of Islam in countries of the Middle East. The welfare system is just as binding to the freedom of people in the United States as the Iron Curtain is to Eastern Europe or the Bamboo Curtain is to Southeast Asia. The dungeon of human misery in which a cancer victim finds himself is just as torturous as the interrogation cell of a mad communist warlord. One death is as bad as the next, for when anyone dies without Jesus Christ, he steps into an eternity without God, and how hopeless and incomprehensible a death this proves to be.

We must tell the captives that Jesus Christ is alive. But Paul asked, "How then shall they call upon Him in Whom they have not believed? And how shall they believe in Him of Whom they have not heard? And how shall they hear without a preacher?" (Rom. 10:14).

I was twenty-one before I heard my first gospel presentation, and I grew up in "Christian" America. At "church," I was raised on ice cream and cookies, but no Jesus—and that's the way it has been for most of us.

God is looking for men and women with the commitment to go and "tell it like it is." He still wonders why so few are willing to stand in the gap, and make up the hedge in "all kinds of prayer" (Eph. 6:18), and in spiritual warfare for those who are dying (Isa. 57:1; Ezek. 22:30; Isa. 59:16). God, the Father, sent God, the Son, to be the Intercessor. Jesus identified with fallen man even to the point of death on a criminal's cross, and the Father raised Him from death and has honored Him at His own right hand. From this position of honor and power Jesus seeks those men and women who will give their lives away in order to see His kingdom come on earth as it is in heaven.

This book comes out of His deep desire to see those men and women come forth with such a display of His glory that the world will stand in total awe of them, and gladly give themselves back to Him.

This book also comes out of my great desire to see God have His way. As remarkable as it may sound, Jesus has bound himself to carrying out His will on the earth through His Church. First Corinthians 12 reveals that in the Body of Christ, the head does not say to the feet, "I have no need of you."

Clearly, Jesus Christ is the head of the Church (Col. 1:18). He is depending upon the various members of His body to commit themselves seriously to the work that lies before them. The writer of the letter to the Hebrews tells us that Jesus is seated at God's right hand, "from henceforth expecting His enemies to be made a footstool for His feet" (Heb. 10:12–13). How can this be done? Through a Church that is one-hundred-percent sold out! Through a people who have given themselves to the training and strict preparation necessary for becoming God's crack commando forces.

This little book can in no way be exhaustive. It is written *to you* with the sincere hope that it will ignite a fire within you that will never be quenched. Perhaps you'll really "hear" for the first time what the Lord is saying to His Church at this hour. If one man or one woman becomes a better-equipped and more-committed Christian because of this book, it will be worthwhile.

I wrote this book because our God is indeed putting together, all over this planet, various assault teams for this crucial hour of human history. I pray that *Kingdom Commandos* will become one of many training manuals, or warfare handbooks, that will be circulated throughout the Body of Christ, and that a serious warrior might be able to gain from it in one week what otherwise might take years.

I also needed to write this book because it has been an ever-growing "fire burning in my bones, and I cannot hold it in any longer" (Jer. 20:9 TLB). God has told me that the effectiveness of this ministry will be enhanced as a result of my making this book available to His people.

In love, sincerity, and humility, I make *Kingdom Commandos* available to you. This is the greatest generation in which to be alive. Rejoice in that fact and seize your destiny in God.

—Malcolm (Chip) Hill, Jr.

1

God's Commandos

Many sincere Christians erroneously believe that unless God
sovereignly chooses to place His mantle of power on them
they are destined to lead a run-of-the-mill life of mediocrity.
They have the idea that great men like the Apostles Paul and
Peter were great only because God made them that way. While
that is true in one sense, we need to realize that these leaders
also had a part to play in their greatness. They made decisions
that contributed to their roles in God's kingdom—decisions
that only they could have made.

Too many are leaving it up to circumstances and the devil to
make decisions for them. Deciding to be *great* for God is one of
your high callings in life. Do not be one of the thousands who
believe they really have no choice.

As I have ministered to the Body of Christ over the years I
have come to see that many believe God has a special "anointing gun" in heaven, and that periodically He chooses some

1

lucky, unsuspecting soul on earth and anoints him greatly. However, this idea is not in good keeping with either Old or New Testament teaching.

While it is true that God has His elite servants within the ranks of His massive spiritual army, it is not true that only those predestined to "elitehood" get to be included in that special number. You have something to say about that, and so have I.

If you desire to be in special service in God's army; if you would be one of the elite of God—then this book is for *you!* It is designed to stir you, to encourage you, and to give you a clearer picture of what God may have available for you and how you can attain it.

The word "elite" drums up the idea of aristocracy—government *by* the rich and *for* the rich. It carries with it the idea of inherited wealth and social position. I picture the wealthy aristocrat who never has to rub elbows with the peons of society. After all, he's above them and better than they are. However, this *is not* what we are talking about when we speak of the elite of God. We are speaking of the choice part—the most carefully selected part of God's total army. There are those in every army who are most likely to succeed in tough or dangerous situations. They always seem to be in the thick of what is happening and seem to receive much commendation from their commanding officers. What makes them different? Were they born with such gifting? No, they weren't, but they have given themselves to spiritual preparation and have trained long and hard in order to be useful.

In many motion pictures we have seen characters who are some of the best special servicemen the military ever produced. They are highly trained experts in guerilla warfare tactics. They do things ordinary men cannot do. These fictional characters, like real-life special servicemen, have trained hard to become the best they can be. It is no different in spiritual things. God is looking for a few good men and women who have the mettle to be His elite ones. Special ministry can only be filled by specialists. God seeks for those He can place in special situations—those He can send behind enemy lines in

2

order to set captives free. A trained commando knows how to slip in undetected and wreak havoc in Satan's camp for God's glory.

There are some who will read this book and will not become elite members of God's commando forces, because they are lazy. But others will never be the same again. How will it be with you, my friend? Can you determine to whip yourself into spiritual shape for this high calling of God? If you can, then you are destined to see His miraculous power at work in your life and through you. You are destined to see Satan's captives go free in Jesus' Name!

That God's eyes "run to and fro throughout the whole earth, seeking to show Himself strong" in the behalf of those few committed ones, and that He seldom finds them, is apparent. See 2 Chron. 16:9 and Ezek. 22:30. It must sadden His great heart that so few will commit their lives to Him in order to be spent for His purposes. The trained commando gives his all to his leader, taking up his cross daily, and following the Lord. He has no misgivings about dying for the cause of His Kingdom. Following the Lord wherever He leads is his reason for living, and he will follow all the more closely in order to see even one captive go free from satanic bondage.

I love to reflect on the incident in Uganda, East Africa, in the late seventies, when an Israeli airliner full of Israeli passengers was held captive at Entebbe Airport by Moslem dictator Idi Amin. This sadistic ruler thought he had the world by the tail, and that Israel in particular was being brought to her knees. But all of a sudden, in a lightning-fast rescue mission carried out by crack Israeli commandos, the hostages were airlifted out of Uganda and Amin didn't even know it was happening until it was too late. Now the world laughs at him.

This world is full of hostages. Multitudes of men, women, and children sit helplessly enslaved by the kingdom of darkness. In this hour of human history God is putting together His crack force of elite kingdom commandos who will storm the very gates and strongholds of hell and set these captives free. Jesus is the leader of these rangers, and as they keep their eyes on Him, He will show them exactly how to succeed in every

3

situation. But they must be instructed by Him and approved before they go forth. It has always been this way.

Now let us look at a few Scriptures that show us God has elite warriors for difficult tasks:

And when Abram heard that his brother [nephew Lot] was taken captive, he armed his trained [instructed] servants, born in his own house, and pursued them unto Dan. (Gen. 14:14)

Notice, they were born in his own house. They were loyal to Abram and he knew them well. He had trained them for warfare and so he knew what they could do. These were special servants whom Abram could trust to get the job done. He obviously had other servants, but he chose to commission his instructed servants.

The Lord always sends instructed servants on special do-or-die missions. The mediocre believer doesn't usually get sent because he has not given himself to the strict training necessary.

Uzziah, king of Judah, at one point during its history, is said to have had a host of fighting men who went out to war by bands. Each band was a crack force of kingdom commandos and they were feared throughout the land. The Word tells us that they made war "with mighty power, to help the king against the enemy" (2 Chron. 26:13). Uzziah's name spread far abroad, for he was *marvelously* helped until he was strong. As with Uzziah, so with Jesus, the King of kings! As we go forth fearlessly in these last days, we can marvelously help Him until His great name is taken to the ends of the earth.

King David of Israel is said to have had a few elite, "mighty men." Strengthening themselves with him in his kingdom, they became men of renown. Adino was the one who lifted his spear to slay 800 men at once. Eleazar defied the Philistines (even when his fellows had fled) and smote them until his hand was heavy. The Lord wrought a great victory through him and the rest of his army did not return until it was time to collect the spoils of the battle.

Then there was Shammah. This man of valor also stood

4

alone during a Philistine attack when all of his men had deserted him and fled. But he stood in the midst of the ground, and defended it, and slew the Philistines; and the Lord wrought another great victory! There were three others who because of their loyalty to their king, broke through enemy lines merely to fetch him a cold drink of water. Abishai was another mighty man of God who lifted his spear against 300 of the enemy. He too made a name for himself, although that is not why he did it—he loved his king. Benaiah single-handedly slew two lion-like men of Moab: he went down also into a pit and slew a lion. On top of these mighty acts, he slew an impressive man of the Egyptians—with the man's own spear! Browse through these exciting verses from 2 Samuel 23 and 1 Chronicles 11. They will increase your vision of valor.

All of the mighty ones of Old Testament times were normal men and women who simply gave themselves wholeheartedly to the service of their king. They were no different from you and me; only God's Spirit anointed them as they gave themselves entirely to what He was doing in the earth. We can have the same results if we will but commit ourselves deeply to His cause.

Let us now consider Gideon's 300 commandos. Gideon numbered the people of God at the Well of Harod in order to give them instruction on how to go out against their enemies in battle. Before he could do anything else God told him to send all of the fearful back home, because they were not fit for the fight. It is a wise thing that he did what God instructed because fear is contagious. Years before, Moses had been instructed to send the fearful home lest the hearts of their brethren faint as well as their hearts (Deut. 20:8). Fear will always put you in reverse, and when you are going backwards you are not moving ahead in what God has planned.

After the fearful departed ten thousand strong remained—ready to go into battle. Or were they ready? Obviously not, because God instructed Gideon to submit them to a simple test in order to determine who the elite really were. As they went to drink out of the Well of Harod, Gideon was instructed to notice the different ways in which the would-be commandos

5

got their drinks. Whoever laid down his weapon in order to drink, was deemed unfit for the battle. All of those who held fast to their weapons with one hand, while bringing water up to their mouths with the other were counted worthy to go out against the enemy.

As a result of this test only 300 commandos remained. There were only three hundred men of God against Midianites and Amalekites who were like grasshoppers for multitude (Judg. 7:12). Perhaps you are thinking: "So few against so many?" Sure, why not? The Bible says there is no restraint to the Lord to save by many or by few (1 Sam. 14:6). The size of the opponent's army doesn't bother the Lord at all—and it shouldn't bother us either. So what if there are myriads of demon spirits operating against us in this world? In Jesus Christ we are absolute masters over every one of them. If our sufficiency is in Christ, and not in ourselves, we have it made. See yourself as a giant killer, and not as a grasshopper, in the fray. Your enemy will be forced to look on you as you look on yourself.

In Numbers 13 we hear the spies who brought up a negative report saying that the giants—the sons of Anak—were so big and fearsome-looking that they felt like grasshoppers before them. Read it for yourself:

> And there we saw the giants, the sons of Anak, which come of the giants: and we were in *our own sight* as grasshoppers, and so we were in their sight. (Num. 13:33, KJV)

Isn't that statement revealing? It is telling us that if we deem ourselves to be mere grasshoppers before our enemies, then that is precisely how they will look upon us. We need to develop, and maintain, a "giant-killer" mentality, and a victory consciousness.

There was a day in my life when a physical giant named rheumatoid arthritis came to lay seige on my body. This debilitating disease worked overtime for a period of four years as it twisted and swelled the various joints of my body. Because I was ignorant of certain undying truths related to

6

the cross of Christ, I figured I was destined to suffer the horrors of the arthritic to my dying day.

The teaching I had received up to that point in my life did very little to prepare me to defend myself against such an imposing giant. I simply laid down before it and allowed it to walk all over me because I saw myself as helpless before it.

However, this story has a happy ending. In the year 1975, God's truth burst into my life and I began to learn that Jesus not only bore my sin on the cross, but He also bore my sickness and disease. Jesus' blood officially redeemed me from the curse of arthritis. By comparing such verses of Scripture as Gal. 3:13 with Deut. 28:22, I saw that arthritis was definately a curse from which I had been redeemed. As I continued to meditate on such eternal truths, and as I made them a part of my daily confession, I began to experience release from the arthritis and its effects.

Today I live as a healed and grateful man. I am grateful because God revealed His truth to me, and I am healed because I received that truth and it has become healing to my bones. No longer do I see myself as a helpless grasshopper before my enemies. As a free and grateful man, I am determined to take God's life-changing principles to my fellow-men who may still be sitting, in fear and bondage to the giants of Satan.

In like manner, as the Body of Christ rises to its feet, arrayed in formidable armor, and carries the fight to the enemy (for a change), the kingdom of darkness will tremble and quake. We need to get on the offensive.

If we are reading the signs of the times accurately, and if our interpretations of such prophetic Scriptures as Ezekiel 38 are correct, the strong-armed powers of communism and Islam are about to be shaken to the teeth. Moscow's iron grip on the masses will be loosened, if not destroyed, and the deluding death grip of the antichrist of Islam will be loosened.

At present, hundreds of millions of people are captured beneath the ungodly paws of these philosophies. When these realms are toppled by God himself, the doors to their lands will be swung wide open to the millions of faithful men and women of God who are at present laboring in prayer, limited opportunity, and elite preparedness. They'll go forth in that hour to swing "the sickle of the Lord" and reap the harvest of the unreached peoples of the world, gathering them into the Kingdom of God. In Revelation 14 we see that this time of reaping will be tremendously intense, and it will be accomplished in an amazingly short period of time. It is time for you who have been asleep to wake up! Do not let this time pass you by. It is even now upon us. The Scriptures say that "He that sleeps in time of harvest is a son that causes much shame" (Prov. 10:5). I don't believe any sincere Christian desires to be a source of shame in this hour, but if we sleep we will be.

It is thrilling to witness what God is doing in the world today. The newspapers make it appear as though the devil has everything going his way; but we must remember he has always made this world's headlines. The truth is that God is winning the war, and you are a part of His winning team!

Iran, Turkey, Iraq, Libya, Ethiopia, Afghanistan, India, and many other countries are about to have their doors opened wide for this glorious gospel. Their masses await a visitation from God!

China has miraculously opened its doors to Jesus. I cannot begin to speculate how long this will last; all I know is that they are open *now* and a great awakening is taking place in China. The revival of New Testament Christianity there is awesome. Tens of millions are coming to know Jesus. Soon other Far Eastern countries will be forced to allow us in, because Satan's hold is weakening in response to the worldwide warfare of the saints.

America and Europe are continuing to ripen for the "special" revival God has told us is coming. Though dead traditionalism and a compromised presentation of the Word of God have taken their toll on the church in the United States and Europe, God is now birthing a "special generation" of men and women who are disgusted with mere form and religion, and are diligently returning to an authentic style of New Testament Christianity not seen since the days of the first apostles. Out of the restored church there will come such a flood of signs and wonders as the world has never seen before, and multitudes will be gloriously swept into the Kingdom of God.

Latin America is experiencing a sweep of God's power that is hard for the natural mind to comprehend. Though communism is claiming the headlines concerning this part of the world, the Kingdom of God is advancing more rapidly as God pours out His spirit on all flesh, just as the Word said He would.

Africa is presently swaying under the weight of the greatest move of God the world has ever witnessed. Even while bad news fills the headlines, millions of Africans are being ushered into God's family. I know, because I've been there and I've seen it firsthand, and I plan to go back. Many top men have been quoted as saying, "If the revival in Africa continues like it is now, the entire continent will be reached by the year 2,000."

The islands of the sea are also being greatly affected. Already, the invasion forces of God have stormed ashore, and have set up impressive spiritual beachheads.

Canada, Egypt, Thailand—no matter where you look, "the fields are ripe and ready for harvesting" (John 4:35).

I recently heard that between 1981 and 1985, in Marxist countries alone, fifty million people received Jesus as their Lord and Savior. Isn't that exciting? Statistics tell us that on this very day seventy-eight thousand people in the world will be reached with the gospel. You can easily see that it has already begun, and it is destined to get better if we will all pull together and do our parts.

A Word to Those Who Feel Left Out.

I exhort those of you who labor strictly on a local level to hold fast to your faith for things to begin happening where you are. Just look around you. Those people who until now have been hardened or indifferent to the gospel, will suddenly acquire an insatiable thirst to know the living God. Do not allow their present reaction to your witness to defeat you. The effect of God's Spirit and Word on the hearts of men and women in these last days is going to be profound. Use your time wisely by preparing, by training hard to become the best you can possibly be. Your diligence will pay off—just wait and see.

2

Behind the Gates of Hell

In a startling discourse with the fisherman Peter, Jesus made the statement that the gates of hell would not prevail (be an adequate defense against) the Church (Matt. 16:18 NAS). This statement actually helped set the attitude the Church was to have toward the work of hell from that point forward. Jesus taught that His mobile, militant Church was to burst actively through the gates of Satan's strongholds, and liberate those held captive within.

Where are these strongholds and their gates? Is He talking figuratively or is He talking literally about storming through the gates of the place called hell? I believe "the gates of hell" (in this verse from the Scriptures) means any place where you find fellow human beings in bondage.

People are in bondage to so many different forces. They are hostages, crying out for deliverance. Bondage to drugs, alcohol, nicotine and caffeine runs rampant throughout society. I am talking about *bondage*—people who cannot quit their harmful habits because they are enslaved.

There are multitudes caught in the web of fornication. Sexual fantasy controls them, driving them to lead promiscuous life styles. I estimate, through years of counseling, that as many as 90 percent of this world's young men are bound by the habit of masturbation (Lev. 15:16–17, 22:4; Deut. 23:10; Gen. 38:9–10). Pornography gazers are everywhere—men who are bound by the exploitative powers of the women (men and children) who "adorn" the filthy pages of the millions of smut magazines bought and sold annually in this country alone. Those enslaved by this industry cannot be set free, apart from the miraculous, liberating power of Jesus Christ of Nazareth! I speak from experience, for Jesus set me free from bondage to pornography. Only He could have done it.

I was first introduced to pornography as a twelve-year-old growing up in middle-class America. I had a newspaper route and every weekday afternoon I would spend about half an hour on a street corner folding papers in preparation for delivery. On that corner were several older paperboys. As we sat there, folding newspapers, the jokes would fly. By the time I was thirteen, I knew every filthy word you can think of. I also learned a great deal about sex although I had not experienced it firsthand.

One day one of the boys brought an X-rated magazine to the corner. I can still remember my first lustful gaze at the unclad women in those pictures. My heart raced and my mind went wild with sexual fantasy. Something diabolical took root in me that day, and it drove me for years to come. An insatiable thirst for pornography consumed me and lust drove me like a fierce wind does a wildfire on the open plains.

When I met Jesus at the age of twenty-two and I gave my life to Him, I somehow knew that the pornography would have to go. But it wasn't that easy.

The compulsion was incessant and unrelenting. Though I dearly loved Jesus and wanted to please Him, the tentacles of pornography and lust were wrapped too tightly around my soul. Actually, I was controlled by an unclean spirit who was determined to retain me as his captive.

12

In His great mercy, God revealed to me the reality of demon spirits, and the authority we, as Christians, have over them. As He established me in that truth, I began to be fed up with that spirit and his intrusion in my life. The day came when I stood to my feet and demanded that spirit to leave me in Jesus' name. He obeyed, and was gone.

In time, I learned the ugly reality that if you drive a demon away he will, at some time in the future, try to regain entrance in your life. I learned that in order to maintain my freedom I would have to stand guard over my soul. Time and time again I had to resist him, and each time he would flee. I learned I had to do away with all forms of temptation with regard to pornography, and so I burned my stack of pornographic magazines.

However, the battle wasn't over yet. I learned that there was another enemy warring in my body, seeking to bring me into captivity to the law of sin. It was the flesh—that hostile old man who was desperately trying to stay free from the absolute Lordship of Jesus. In order for me to see total victory I would have to root him out and crucify him. It was accomplished through much fasting and prayer and telling my body what it could and could not do.

I also submitted by struggles to a Christian brother to whom I could make myself accountable. His prayer support and encouragement were invaluable.

All of these things, together with much crying out to God, were what set me free from bondage. Now I believe I am in a very special place of ministry for men and boys who are at present in the bondages that once enslaved me.

Pre-marital sex is also rampant in society. Folks are not only bound by it—they like it! Adultery also holds millions in its clutches, and once someone begins an adulterous life style, it is next to impossible for him or her to stop. Where are the gates of hell? Perhaps right next door to you. Perhaps right in your own house.

One in two marriages ends in divorce. Marriages all around you are sick, because romantic love has lost its novelty and thrill, and the marriage partners are ignorant of the fact that when they entered into marriage they entered into a covenant with one another, and therefore must grit their teeth and work

13

things out. Instead, they quickly shuck the whole thing. These folks are listed in Romans one: Covenant breakers!

Couples live together out of wedlock because they are not persuaded that the marriage covenant is the only way to live with one another. The Bible calls them implacable (Rom. 1:31) ". . . those who cannot be persuaded to enter into a covenant" (Vines, pg. 590).

Hospitals and mental institutions are filled with sick and broken people. They need God's commandos to make lightning-fast raids into their situations and bring the power of God to set them free.

The poor need the gospel preached to them. Jesus said they would always be with us, so we have no excuses. The gospel (or good news) to the poor man is that if he will turn his life entirely over to Jesus, God will begin to meet every one of his needs. Poverty is a curse, and Jesus came to deliver us from its power.

Deceptions and delusions of all sorts hold untold millions in darkness. They desperately need the glorious light of the gospel to shine upon them. The god of this world, Satan, has blinded their minds so they cannot see through the darkness.

The demonic spirits of fear torment people everywhere. Most people have no idea that the fears and phobias that haunt them are really needless irritations that the manifest power and authority of God can easily overcome. But if they do not know these things, they remain in torment.

I think by now you can see where the gates of hell are—all around you. Perhaps the clerk behind the check-out counter at the local market is imprisoned behind these gates, or the little, old lady who lives across the street, and is being crippled by a spirit of arthritis. The child up the street who has no one who truly cares. The couple at the edge of town who are about to lose their marriage of eighteen years. The list goes on and on—captives in the tormenting prisons of the enemy.

Regardless of the particular arena of warfare into which you find God leading you, see to it that you wage war determinedly and scripturally. Your determination is to win, and to do it according to the Word of God. Whether you experience victory in one fell swoop, or by attrition, see to it that you win—and that you win decisively.

Realize that no two situations can be approached in exactly the same way. Although the gifts of the Spirit (1 Cor. 12) are the same, the operations of these gifts may vary greatly. Jesus anointed one man's eyes with spittle, but He healed another blind man by simply speaking His word. He raised one from the dead by taking hold of her hand and gently saying, "arise," while at another time He commanded with a loud voice, "Lazarus, come forth!" Be led by the One who knows what the heart of the Father is for each situation. Even Jesus said, "I only do what I see the Father doing" (John 5:19). The Holy Spirit has been given us to show the way of the Father, to tell us the way of the Father, and to enable us to do the work of the Father.

When dealing with multitudes of people and the myriads of problems they possess, you must be in fine tune with the Spirit of God. You must sometimes refute others so as to convince them with argument and evidence, as Paul did in Athens, Corinth, and on Cyprus. To others you must show mercy (on those who waver and doubt). Still for others you must strive (fight) in order to snatch them from the very fires of compromise, defeat, and eventual hell. Different people are to be dealt with in different ways.

> For example, there was one man I tried to win to the Lord for years. Every time I confronted him I tried the gentle approach. I was soft-spoken and only inserted some gospel when he was in a good mood and the perfect opportunity was present. In all those years I got nowhere with him. One day I felt impressed to try a different approach. I walked boldly into his house, catching him in a bad mood, and loudly declared, "If you don't repent and receive Jesus soon, you're gonna split hell wide open!"

> His first reaction was anything but favorable, but time proved that my word to him, blunt though it was, was what jarred him to his senses and brought him to Christ. Within the week he was seized with such a realization of impending judgment that he humbly and reverently asked Jesus to forgive him and come into his heart.

The very opposite of this example has proven effective many other times. Gentle, caring words spoken in due season, have brought great men to their knees in humble submission to Christ.

I have seen a gentle whisper send demons fleeing, and I have experienced times when the name of Jesus, shouted at the top of one's lungs, was barely sufficient to break a stubborn demon's cruel reign over a poor soul's life.

Whatever it takes, we must be ready to follow the Spirit's leading in order to see victory. We must be open to doing things in different ways or our ministries will be greatly limited. Once I settled this issue for myself the victories became commonplace. Jesus told me that I must be willing to appear "wild" if the need for it arose. He told me that if I wasn't so willing then He would not be able to send "impossible cases" to me for deliverance.

There are some spirits who will not respond to a gentle pat on their victims hands and a "God bless you, brother. . . . I'll be in prayer for you concerning your problem." I literally had to grab a demon-oppressed person by the shoulders and shake him while commanding the spirit to leave, and on the other hand, I have seen a gentle whisper do the job.

A long time ago I heard Bible teacher and evangelist Norvel Hayes relate how he and Lester Sumrall were in a motel restaurant having a cup of coffee after a meeting one night. He said a young woman, controlled by a spirit of lesbianism, approached him and before she could open her mouth to say anything to him, she hauled off and slapped him across the face. She had been in the meeting where he and Lester had preached earlier and though she was inwardly crying out for freedom, the spirit controlling her had been greatly agitated.

Norvel leaped to his feet, grabbed the poor, bound soul, and cast her to the floor. He yelled, "You foul spirit controlling this woman, come out of her in Jesus' name. Come out, I said, in Jesus' name!" She was immediately set free from that bondage, gloriously saved and launched into her Christian walk. That kind of action is not the normal way of casting out demons; it is the exception. But when the Holy Spirit leads the deliverance minister in doing it that way, he had better obey. Anything less may result in defeat.

16

Behind the gates of hell are masses of suffering humanity. You are the very one God desires to send into their midst and work a great deliverance. Your mind set has to be that there must be a wholesale extermination of the demon forces holding the people of the world in darkness. It begins in your neighborhood and extends to the whole world. You are a "cut above," and definitely a "breed apart," and God is sending you in this special climax of history as we know it, to turn many to righteousness—"to open their eyes, and turn them from darkness to light, and from the power of Satan unto God, that they may receive forgiveness of sins, and an inheritance among those who have been sanctified by faith in Jesus Christ" (Acts 26:18).

3

Where Do You Begin?

You begin with a quality decision. You must choose to be the best special-forces Christian you can possibly be. And get this straight: You don't need worldwide recognition in order to be one of the elite of God!

There was a time early in my Christian life when I told God I wanted to be right on the front lines of what He was doing in the earth. I still want that; I am still asking Him for that too. And guess what? I'm there. No, I don't have worldwide fame in the Body of Christ. I don't need that. All I need is to open my eyes and look on the harvest fields of the world where people live in scriptural ignorance. Satan has used their ignorance and has deceived them into thinking there is no way out of their situations. They do not know that the traps in which they sit are broken.

> Our soul [whole being] is escaped as a bird out of the snare of the fowlers: *the snare is broken,* and we are escaped. (Ps. 126:7, italics mine)

On the cross, Jesus disarmed principalities and their realms of authority. He triumphed over Satan and his entire kingdom. Jesus took from Satan all the armor in which he trusted and spoiled his house—spoiled his kingdom. Jesus walked Satan's trap line and broke every one of his traps (See Col. 2:15; Luke 11:21–22).

All around us are people who have believed the lie from hell that they are enslaved in bondages from which they cannot be freed. What a job it is to go to them and tell them the good news. What a thrill to witness the manifest power of God as He sets them free.

Another essential in preparing yourself for your Commander's use is found in some advice Paul gave to Timothy:

> Thou therefore endure hardness, as a good soldier of Jesus Christ. No man that warreth entangleth himself with the affairs of this life; that he may please Him Who hath chosen him to be a soldier. (2 Tim. 2:3,4)

In order to become a good soldier you will have to strip many things from your schedule. Jesus said that the responsibilities of this age, the desires for other things, and the deceitfulness of riches, enter into the would-be follower of His, and choke the Word out of the heart (Mark 4:19).

I know of Christian men who are absolutely enslaved by their jobs. Their bondage to work, coupled with an uncontrolled lust for material possessions, cripples them before the enemy of their souls. Unable to tend to the Word of God and prayer in their lives, they become useless in the Body of Christ. An insatiable thirst for more and better of this world's playthings forces them to slave at a second and third job in order to pay their bills and make ends meet. How deplorable this is, and how it must sadden the heart of a holy God who has called us into His kingdom's service.

Still other men, who could do better, are bound by giving all of their free time to the pursuit of a sport or hobby. What a joke they are as they present themselves and their families to Satan. Fun and pleasure have superseded the duty of keeping themselves spiritually sharp and prepared for any future conflict with Satan's kingdom.

I think you get my point. These men, who would be serving in the trenches with me, are not merely letting me down—they are letting Jesus down.

The soldier must also be one who is able to endure hardness, able to bear up under the heavy load of commitment to the Kingdom of God. If you will become one of the elite in God's army, you will have to show your willingness to Him to press through the cleverly devised obstacle courses He'll set before you. You will have to wrestle the angel for the blessing, just as Jacob had to, because God wants to see if you truly mean business.

The letters Paul wrote to Timothy are rich in important commando instruction. They are wartime letters. Read what Paul wrote to Timothy, an upcoming commando:

> Study to show yourself approved unto God, a workman that needeth not to be ashamed, accurately handling the Word of Truth. (2 Tim. 2:15)

You will not make it in God's special forces if you are not a diligent student of the Word of God. If you don't study to make the Word a part of your innermost being, you will suffer much shame as you seek to operate behind enemy lines. I tell you from experience that a cultist who knows his stuff, will "chew you up, and spit you out." You must be diligent to "hide the Word in your heart" (Ps. 119:11), so that when you are under pressure it will just naturally come out of your mouth in order to withstand the attack of the enemy.

David said, "Let my heart be sound in Thy statutes; that I be not ashamed (Ps. 119:80). Your heart becomes sound as you diligently fill it with the Word of God.

A good friend of mine was in a heated discussion with an adherent of the Bahai Faith a couple of years ago, and at one point the Bahai follower accused Christians of being narrow-minded. Immediately, my friend retaliated with a verse from Matthew where Jesus said, "Narrow is the way, and straight is the gate that leads to life everlasting." The Bahai member was flabberghasted! This is a good example of being prepared to do battle.

The well-known evangelist T.L. Osborn was preaching in a

country where Islam is strong. At one point during his campaign, an Islamic priest approached him with this challenge, "The book that you preach from is not the Word of God, but my Koran is!" T.L. could have stood there all day and into the night and argued the point, and probably would have gotten nowhere. But he didn't. He quickly called forward a multitude of deaf and blind folks and challenged Allah's priest to pray for them and heal them. The Muslim would not do it because he knew nothing would happen. So T.L. prayed for them in the Name of the living Lord Jesus, whom the Bible teaches, and God's power healed all but a few of them. T.L. then challenged the Muslim priest to worship the God of the Bible—the One who is truth! God does not want us to be ashamed as we go forth to liberate the captives.

The Muslim priest, and all who witnessed this display of God's power, went from there that day knowing who the one true God is. Because T.L. Osborne had prepared through study, he knew Him who is right, and true, and all-powerful. T.L. knew that Jesus Christ is the same, yesterday, and today, and forever, and by proclaiming Jesus' Word, he would not be put to shame.

Study the Word of God in order to see how Jesus and His followers responded to the many different situations that arose in their ministries.

Study the biographies of great men and women of God who blazed trails before your time. Learn from their successes, as well as their failures. Men and women like C. T. Studd, Hudson Taylor, Gladys Aylward, George Mueller, Smith Wigglesworth, Lillian Yeomans, Rees Howells, and many others. This is essential to your becoming a successful commando in Jesus' army.

Another area of preparation in which you must involve yourself is the school of "weapons." Any outstanding commando is an expert in the use of his weapons. He knows them well, and is highly efficient in making them work for him. One reason why so many believers have become casualties in the conflicts of life is because they have not taken the time to master their weapons.

In the natural army, a recruit must go through boot camp in order to become prepared for future battle. One requirement in boot camp is that the soldier become so familiar with his weapons that he be able to disassemble and reassemble them in the dark. Suppose he is in a muddy trench or a foxhole at some point in his military career and during the heat of nighttime battle his gun becomes clogged with mud? Let's say the firing mechanism has to be taken apart before it can be freed. If the soldier does not know how to break his weapon down he is at a tremendous disadvantage. He must be adept at tearing his weapon down, correcting the problem, and reassembling it before his enemy finds him weaponless.

Suppose the soldier is limited in his knowledge of available weapons? Let's say he knows how to operate only an M-16 machine gun, but knows nothing at all about the use of a rocket launcher. Knowledge of the M-16 is great, but let's face it—the M-16 will not do in every situation.

It is this way in spiritual warfare too.

We've been given weapons that are mighty through God to the pulling down of strongholds (2 Cor. 10:4). Another translation says that they're useful for the "overthrow and destruction of fortresses!" I love that! Through proper use of proper weapons at the proper time, we can storm and plunder the very strongholds of Satan, where so many fellow human beings are being held captive.

What are the Christian's weapons? Because so much has already been written concerning the weapons God has issued to the Christian, I will not spend much time on their use. However, I would be remiss if I were not to name them for you. After you discover what they are, I suggest you study the Bible for yourself to see how they are to be used, and then read the wealth of material on this topic available in Christian bookstores.

Our spiritual weapons are:

1. The Word of God. (See Heb. 4:12; Luke 4:3–13)
2. The Blood of Jesus. (See Rev. 12:11; Eph. 1:7; Ps. 107:2)
3. The Word of our testimony. (Rev. 12:11). Testify vocally

as to what God's Word says the blood of Jesus does for you.

4. The Name of Jesus. (See Mark 16:17–18; Acts 16:16–18; Acts 3:6 and 16)

In warfare, most weapons must be fired, launched, dropped, thrown, or thrust. The most powerful weapons have to reach their targeted destinations. Thank God, we have ways of getting our weapons where they are needed. They are:

1. Prayer. (Acts 4:18–31, 12:1–7; Ps. 55:9 TLB)
2. Praise. (Acts 16:25; Ps. 149; 2 Chron. 20:21–22)
3. Testimony. (Acts 26:28)
4. Preaching. (1 Cor. 1:21; Luke 4:16–21, 5:1,15, 6:17; Rom. 10:14)
5. Teaching. (Matt. 5:23; 9:35)
6. Decree. (Authoritative order backed with the force of law—See Job 22:28; Mark 11:23; Acts 16:18)

The power needed to make all of this effective is the power of the Holy Spirit. Ephesians 3:20 says that this power works within us. Why? Because the Holy Spirit is within us! He is a person, and He operates in us, causing rivers of living water to gush out of us unto needy humanity (John 7:37–39).

It is essential for the soldier of God to be filled with the Holy Spirit. I'm not talking about being *born* of the Spirit, but *filled* with the Spirit.

Two people can line up to pray the same prayer. One is filled with the Spirit of God and the other one isn't. The one who is not filled with the Spirit probably won't get the answer, while the one who is filled with the Spirit will. How can this be? Because Eph. 3:20 says very clearly, "God is able to do exceeding abundantly above all that we *ask* or think, according to *the power* that works within us" (italics mine). This goes to show that true prayer is not just saying a bunch of words. The Spirit of God must be intimately involved.

This holds true in prayer, praise, testimony, preaching and teaching, or in decree: it's according to the power that works in you! That is why Paul told the believers to "be ever filled and stimulated with the Spirit'' (Eph. 5:18 TAB). This is the responsibility of the believer, not of God!

Another aspect of readying yourself for elite kingdom assignment is found in Ephesians 6, concerning the whole armor of God. We are told that *we* must put it on. God has made it available; we put it on! If we fail to do it, then we will definitely become casualties. I see countless Christians around me who are casualties, because they failed to heed God's instructions to put on the armor.

I remember an experience I had years ago when all of these things were brand-new to me. A pastor friend and I went to minister to a woman who was dying with a terminal disease. She had been a professing Christian for many years, so we automatically assumed that she knew her Bible through and through. As we sat down to share with her, we came to realize that she actually knew very little.

She believed that the Lord had placed the disease on her and that He was seeking glory in her misery. I read to her from Ephesians 6, where Paul talks about the whole armor of God, and how we are to put it on. Before I could finish reading the passage she turned to her husband and asked him in a rather confused tone of voice, "Is that in my Bible?"

She was one of many thousands who scrape through life ignorant of the fact that God has made His impenetrable armor available to His children. Without the armor of God in place, God's children are vulnerable to Satan's attacks, and are likely to end up as casualties. We left her house that day greatly saddened over the fact that she was unable to grasp the essential truths we offered her. She died several months later, another victim of "the famine of the hearing of the Word of God" that was so prevalent in the land.

That, coupled with her age, caused her to be far-too-inflexible for God to do anything with. That is why it is so important to establish people in these essential biblical truths while they are young and pliable. Help the young to get suited-up in the whole armor of God before they face the enemy in the vicious warfare that often accompanies old age.

God's word to the younger generation is this: "Remember now thy Creator in the days of thy youth, while the evil days come not, nor the years draw nigh, when thou shalt say, I have no pleasure in them" (Eccles. 12:1).

The Word of God clearly teaches that if we are diligent to "remember" our Creator by an ever growing fellowship with Him in His Word, and in prayer, then we can one day go to our graves in a full age, like as a shock of corn comes in its season (Job 5:26). When we reach the latter years of our life it is God's desire that we "still bring forth fruit in old age" (Ps. 92:14), and that we be ever abounding in the work of the Lord.

In analyzing the armor piece by piece, you will better understand how to put it on. And remember, it must be worn *daily*.

1. *The belt of truth,* or as the King James Version puts it— "Your loins girt about with the truth." The belt of truth is nothing short of the Word of God having preeminence in every thing you say or do. The Word must be there in order to hold all the rest in place. Without a belt, your pants will fall down. While you're bending over to pull your pants back up, Satan will slice your head off. Also, if your pants fall down around your knees, you'll be stumbling wherever you go. This is why it's so important for you to study the Bible. I have heard people just stumble through difficult situations, and stumble around with unscriptural prayer, because they didn't know what the Word said.

God demanded that Job "Gird up your loins like a man!" (Job 38:2–3). Job had been stumbling about in his deplorable situation because he kept darkening, counsel by word without knowledge. His loins weren't girded with the Word of God. Peter exhorted us to "Gird up the loins of our minds" (1 Pet. 1:13). *Cruden's Concordance* says, "Let your minds be intent upon, ready, and prepared for, your spiritual service." The only way for this to take place is by much diligent study in the Word of God, so that you might have your mind renewed by the truth which is found therein (Rom. 12:2).

The importance of the Scriptures? "That the man of

26

God may be perfect, throughly furnished and prepared for every good work" (2 Tim. 3:17). Hallelujah! Gird up your loins with the truth.

2. *The breastplate of righteousness.* The significance of the breastplate is that it protects your heart and other vital organs. At the core of the Christian's being is the fact that he is "accepted in the beloved." Because of what Jesus did at Calvary, the Christian is "righteous." This means right standing before God. If he weren't righteous, he couldn't be heard on high. He couldn't begin to go out in battle against Satan, "the accuser of the brethren" (Rev. 12:10). Put on the breastplate of righteousness daily, so that when Satan levels his accusations at you, when he condemns and badgers you with past sins, you can rise above it all and thank God for the blood of Jesus, which cleanses you and keeps you in right standing with your heavenly Father.

This righteousness that protects the heart is, as 1 Thessalonians 5:8 says, faith and love, or, faith that is expressed through love.

Put on the breastplate of righteousness or you'll become a casualty.

3. *Good news shoes.* The King James Version says, "Feet shod with the preparation of the gospel of peace."

Notice the word "preparation." You must be prepared to go forth with the good news that Jesus saves, heals, and delivers. The gospel is the "power of God unto salvation" (Rom. 1:16), and as you go forth in Jesus' Name, you must not only have the right words, but also the power to back them up (1 Cor. 2:4–5).

Evangelist Kenneth Copeland relates an incident he was involved in after a meeting he had conducted one afternoon in Florida. He said that he was headed across the parking lot to his car when a little black woman approached him carrying a little baby who was very visibly deformed in its feet and ankle bones. Standing before Kenneth, she simply handed her baby to him, pleading for his prayer of healing with sincere and longing eyes. As he took the little one into his strong Texas hands and began to pray he actually felt the miracle take place.

"I had only begun to pray," he reflected. "The only words I said were, 'Father, in the name of Jesus' and I actually felt the deformed feet and ankle bones straighten out in my hands." Copeland went on to comment that at moments like this, one better be "prayed up" already. Then is not the time to go and "tank up" on the Word of God in order to meet the challenge. If you are not already filled with the Word and operating out of a strong prayer life you will faint in heart, and be defeated by the challenge.

Can you see the importance of staying prepared? God desires to sprinkle challenging situations similar to the one just described through the life of every born-again believer. Sadly, too few are equal to the challenge, and the opportunity, because they are ill-prepared.

How is it with you? If someone were to approach you with a problem similar to the one that was presented to Copeland would you be able to respond in faith?

Are you ready to lead someone to Christ at any hour of any day?

Are opportunities to glorify Jesus passing you by because you are not prepared to field them, and make the most of them? If so, make today a new beginning by giving yourself to God in the Word and in prayer so as to be prepared for the unique opportunities that await you.

The late faith pioneer Smith Wigglesworth was once asked what the secret of his phenomenal miracle ministry was. He simply replied "I give at least two hours to the Lord each morning in prayer and in the Word, get edified myself, and then go out that day and edify the people." Smith was talking about preparation, and we can all prepare.

4. *The shield of faith.* Paul says, "Above all!" Take this one—above all. In the days of Paul the Roman soldier carried a full-body shield that was covered with thick leather. Just prior to battle, he would soak it in water in

order to have the leather shield-covering saturated. This was because his enemies would often dip their arrowheads in pitch and light them. Then they would fire the flaming arrows at the Roman soldiers, but the leather-bound shield, soaked thoroughly in water, would quench the flaming arrows every time.

How does this apply to us in spiritual warfare? As a Christian, your shield is the shield of faith—faith in God's Word! This is nothing short of a consistent, bold confession of that Word. The shield is your confession, soaked in the Word of God! (Notice: we have God's assurance that we will be able to quench *all* the fiery darts or flaming arrows of the enemy. It is God's intention that not one accomplish its mission.)

5. *The helmet of salvation.* Headgear is all important. The helmet of salvation is designed to protect the mind.

The Bible tells the Christian that he has the mind of Christ (1 Cor. 2:16b). This means that potentially we know all things, because Jesus knows all things. I don't believe the Father is keeping anything from Jesus now that He has been glorified and sits at His right hand. The mind and counsel of Jesus Christ is available to the Body of Christ. Proverbs 2:7 tells us that He "lays up sound wisdom *for* the righteous," not "*from* him." The wisdom of God is hidden from the sinner, but not from the righteous. So you see that potentially we are perfectly sharp, mentally!

This is why we need a helmet of salvation. To protect our minds. The battleground for most all conflict with the devil begins in the mind. If you can whip him in the mind, you'll win the battle! How do you whip him in the mind? By strong faith in the Word of God. Refuse to allow Satan's lies and damaging suggestions to linger in your mind. Reign in life by Jesus Christ, and bring every thought into captivity to the obedience of Christ (2 Cor. 10:5). Make every thought line up with what God says concerning your situation. If it doesn't line up with the truth, reject it!

29

Satan's lies, and deceitful suggestions come to us all, but we don't have to allow them to linger. As Kenneth Hagin said, "You can't keep the birds from flying over your head, but you can keep them from nesting in your hair."

When a demon shoots a pain into your body, and suggests that you're getting sick, come forth immediately with the Word of God. Recall that Word. There should be a rich deposit of it in your heart. Meditate on that Word. Confess that Word boldly. Control your mind with the helmet of salvation.

6. *The sword of the Spirit*. The sword of the Spirit is the Word of God. Notice, he said "take the sword of the Spirit." You must *take it*. God won't take it up for you. But praise be to God, as you take it, the Holy Spirit will empower it!

Another thing that is important here is the Greek word translated "Word." It is "rhema," and in this case, it means the "spoken Word of God." Your sword is not the Bible on the bookshelf, not the Bible on the coffee table, but it is the Word spoken out of your mouth against the enemy. Jesus demonstrated this in Luke 4 when Satan came to tempt Him.

Jesus Effectively Arrested Satan With the Spoken Word!

I shared with you how I fought tremendous battles with pornography and arthritis and won. But I want to say that in order to remain free I must stand in God's armor continually. Just because I defeated Satan in the past does not mean I can relax now or in the future. As long as I am in this world I will be in the midst of hostile forces. Satan's troops will come again and try to make me their captive, but I will wield the sword of the Spirit and remain free. Jesus used God's Word as an offensive weapon and successfully repelled Satans' every attack. We can do the same.

There was a time when I grew lazy when it came to speaking the Word of God. The novelty of faith's confession wore off and I was no longer maintaining a solid front. When various adverse circumstances would arise I would not speak the Word audibly. I would only "think" the Scriptures and attempt to repel the enemy with mental gymnastics. It never worked. Then one day as I was reading in Luke 17. I came across these words from Jesus:

"If ye had faith as a grain of mustard seed, ye might say unto this sycamine tree, Be thou plucked up by the root, and be thou planted in the sea; and it should obey you."

As I went to the literal Greek I discovered that the text says that if I have faith *I would say* unto this sycamine tree. It didn't say that *might* or that *I would think*. It called for verbal action. I was to be actively involved in changing my circumstances by speaking words. The Scriptures also tell us that we are to "hold fast to our confession of faith without wavering" (Heb. 10:23). I had not only wavered, but I had stopped altogether my confession of the Word of God. It didn't take me long to correct the problem.

As we examined the armor we are to wear in battle, did you notice that there was no armor to protect your back? This is because God always intends for us to be on the offensive—always advancing. If you turn tail and retreat, you automatically become vulnerable. Don't retreat—go forward and be aggressive! As you go, you can rest assured that the "Glory of the Lord will be your rear guard" (Isa. 58:8).

Wear the armor as you launch offensives against the gates of hell. Satan will not sit idly by and allow you to plunder his house. He'll resist you, and even launch counter-offensives. But be of much courage; "No weapon formed against you will prosper" (Isa. 54:17). You will go into impossible situations, where people seem hopelessly bound, and see them set free. As Jesus did, you'll get in, and you'll get out again, and bring a multitude of former captives with you. Hallelujah!

Still another prerequisite to your becoming an elite member of God's commando forces is that you develop and maintain a consistent life of prayer. Jesus said, "Men ought always to pray, and not faint" (Luke 18:1). Prayer is so important because it helps to keep your mind focused on Jesus. Hebrews 12:3 tells us to "consider Jesus," or "focus on Jesus, lest we be wearied and faint in our minds."

If you do not begin and maintain a life of prayer, I promise that you will faint. You will not make it in God's elite forces apart from diligent prayer.

One prayer warrior said, "Men of prayer must be men of steel, for they will be assaulted by Satan even before they assault his kingdom." I might add, men of steel are only those who are men of prayer! And yes, often Satan will assault you before you assault him. He came against Jesus in the very beginning of His ministry, while He was still in the wilderness, praying and fasting.

Another thing you need to know about prayer is that it is not monologue. You are not to monopolize the conversation. True prayer is dialogue—both parties conversing in a give-and-take discussion.

You are to talk, but you are to take time to be still and listen to God too. He speaks to you in His still, small voice.

Faithfulness is another thing God looks for in a would-be commando. If it is not there, God will not include you in "heavy-duty" rescue operations.

Are you a man or woman of your word? If you tell someone that you'll be at a certain place by 10:00 AM, do you usually get there at ten minutes after 10:00? If so, that's not good enough.

Often, in natural warfare, the members of a commando team must approach a target from different directions at the exact same moment. They synchronize their watches to insure that they will all strike at the exact moment planned. Unfaithfulness on the part of one man can foul up the entire mission, and even cost some folks their lives.

I am a firm believer that the same holds true in many aspects of spiritual warfare. Suppose God instructs me and a brother to converge on the home of a very confused person at 7:00 on a particular Thursday night, in order to show him our concern, God's love, and the truth the Bible reveals in the relaxed atmosphere of his own home. Our Commander, Jesus, has told us to go to him together, that together we would be received. The appointed time rolls around, and my fellow commando isn't there yet. I'm sitting out in my car in front of the confused person's house waiting for the brother so we can go in together. Then 7:30 rolls around, and he still hasn't come. At 8:00, I notice three strangers entering the man's house. He seems to welcome them in. At 8:15 my fellow-commando finally pulls in, apologizing for his tardiness, stating in a sheepish voice, "I laid down after supper to watch the news, and fell asleep." I tell him we had better not go in because at 8:00 the man received some company and we don't want to be rude by interrupting their visit. My fellow-commando and I part that night by saying "We'll do it tomorrow night." We never do rescue the guy from his confusion, because we later find out that the three visitors he had received were Jehovah's Witnesses, and that very night, while I was waiting for my fellow-commando, the three cultists converted him to their beliefs and hopelessly ensnared his soul.

Would you ever promote the tardy commando in the things of God if it were left up to you? I certainly wouldn't, and I don't think God would either! You can't make those kinds of mistakes and expect to win a war. God needs faithful men and women. The Word states:

> Confidence in an unfaithful man in time of trouble is like a broken tooth, and a foot out of joint. (Prov. 25:19)

Who needs him? Who wants him?

Be faithful with your word, God's Word, your money, your time, your energy, and your attitudes and motives. Prove to God that you're a soldier who can be trusted, *then* maybe He will promote you into His commando forces.

I have noticed how God challenges my faithfulness. It has been very easy for me to say that I will do whatever He shows me to do, but actually doing it is sometimes easier said than done. There was the time years ago, for example, when I read from Matthew 5:23 that if you are at the altar, presenting a gift to God, and you remember a brother who has something against you than you are to leave your gift before the altar, and go and be reconciled to your brother, and then come and offer your gift. That was hard for me to deal with. I had had a falling out with a local pastor and things were not right between us. It seems everything I was doing was going awry. At that time in my life I was a beef cattle and sheep farmer. My calves and lambs were dying all around me. A plague ran rampant through my herds—stealing, killing, and destroying. All of my prayers of faith seemed to be bouncing off of heavens of brass, and all of the commands I directed at the enemy were falling far short. Tremendous despair and discouragement engulfed me and I even began to lay the blame on God. One day I watched another lamb die. It was all I could stand. Picking its lifeless body up in my hands, I lifted it high over my head before God and cried out "Why? Don't you care about this, Lord? Why are you letting this happen to me?" At that moment, for the first time in several weeks, I was able to hear what God had been trying to tell me all along: *I had to go and make things right with my brother.*

Here was a clear challenge. I knew what the Word of God instructed me to do, but would I be able to be faithful to it? It meant that I would have to humble myself before someone I thought to be wrong and ask his forgiveness. Up to that time in my life I had never done anything like that before. I wanted to protect myself—I didn't want anyone to think that I might be wrong. But God was calling for faithfulness, and besides a plague was destroying my means of making a living.

I gritted my teeth and went to the brother to ask for his forgiveness. That day will stand out in my memory for all eternity. God's strength accompanied me all the way into town that day and as the pastor and I talked, we were gloriously restored to friendship, and a greater understanding of each other.

When I got home later that day, I discovered that the plague that had been running rampant through my herds had stopped. God saw my faithfulness to obey His Word, and Sovereignly stepped in to stay the plague. I don't even like to think what might have happened to my farming operation had I not been faithful.

Since that time I have had many more opportunities to prove myself faithful. By God's grace, and by a determination to please Him with my life, I have always endeavored to be consistently faithful in what God has shown me to do.

No, it hasn't always been easy to be a faithful servant. It hasn't always been easy to be a man of my word, and there have been times when I have blown it. But by and large, I've been faithful to my God and the call He has placed on my life. He has honored that faithfulness by bringing me up the ladder of success in His kingdom's work. And you, my brother or sister, must also determine that you will be faithful to do all God is calling you to.

"He who is faithful in little things shall be worthy of being entrusted with much."

Something that goes right along with faithfulness is loyalty. Are you loyal to your God and the call He has placed upon your life? If not, forget ever being used much by Him.

One way to prove your loyalty to God is by being loyal to the people with whom you serve and the leadership He's called you to serve under. If you are unable to be loyal to the man or men whom God has called you to serve, then you'll never experience promotion from God. As a pastor, the thing I look for in younger Christians who are aspiring to action or even a leadership role in the warfare, is loyalty to me as their leader. If they can't trust me, if they can't be submissive to my desires as the God-appointed team leader, then they can forget promotion from me—and from God! I'd just as soon they'd get on another man's team.

You can't be loyal to someone, and at the same time say bad things about him behind his back. If you see a problem, loyalty says to go straight to the individual and talk to him about it. If you don't, but continue to talk about him to everyone else, you become a disloyal traitor, not worthy of any consideration at all. Be loyal and go to the person.

If you are truly loyal to someone, you'll bend over backwards to make that person look good. You'll give yourself to his success. You'll esteem him much more highly than you esteem yourself (Phil. 2:3). And God will honor it.

I would be remiss if I were to talk about prerequisites to commando service and leave out the word "resilience." A good commando is a resilient person. The word resilient means, "to bounce or spring back into shape or position."

35

The very fact that you are an elite commando of God, tells us that you find yourself in hard, trying situations at many times in life. You are one of the most dangerous people in the universe where Satan and his kingdom are concerned, and he is out to stop you dead in your tracks. He will apply pressures to you that would break ordinary people. These pressures on your mind, body, and spirit are designed to steal, kill, and destroy (John 10:10). You'll find yourself being pushed to the point where you feel you are about to cave in and collapse. There will be pressure that seems to be pulling at you from every direction, stretching you almost to the breaking point. God will be there to deliver you, and bear you up. It will sometimes appear as though His deliverance came just in the nick-of-time. Nevertheless, at these times, you must spring back into shape and proper form quickly, because the war isn't over yet—you've simply come through another skirmish. After having done all, you are to stand (Eph. 6:13), and be ready to go at it again if you have to. God's power is there to see you through.

Flexibility is an essential requirement in order for you to be a good commando. A slogan I've adopted, and one worthy of remembering from here on out is, "Constant change is here to stay." You need to know that too.

In warfare, situations and circumstances can change minute by minute. You might have it all figured out today, and by tomorrow you'll have to modify your plans because circumstances changed during the night. You may have planned an all-out offensive on the enemy's northern front at daylight tomorrow, only to find out that they got wind of your plan and evacuated their troops during the darkness of the night. What will you do now? Will you be one of those who says, "Bless God, I'm gonna do it as planned because that's the way my granddaddy said it ought to be done!" or, are you going to play it smart and look for a plan that will work? God's Word says:

> Remember ye not the former things, neither consider the things of old. Behold, I will do a new thing; now it shall spring forth; shall ye not know it? I will even make a way in the wilderness, and rivers in the desert. (Isa. 43:18,19)

God is a God of newness. *While it's true that He never contradicts His Word, He is constantly contradicting the traditions of men.* I want to be able to flow along with each new thing the Lord is doing, lest I stagnate and find myself one day fighting against Him.

Many good fighting men have been prematurely removed from the field of battle simply because they were unable to flow with the new plan God was implementing. It is a blessing to see men who are old war-horses in God's army, flowing from wave to wave, as God continues doing new things in order to bring His bride to maturity.

A mistake many in Pentecostal circles made back in the middle parts of this century, and some still make today, is to pray for revival according to *their* terms. When the charismatic movement began, it was revival, but not by Pentecostal terms, so, many Pentecostals bad-mouthed it and found themselves resisting a valid move of God. Many of these folks were removed from the arena of warfare so as not to be a hindrance.

Let us learn from our forerunners' mistakes and allow God to be God. Be flexible.

I would like to close this chapter by exhorting you to become a *team* player. So many Christians are out to have their own big ministry, and they really don't care who they step on to get it. Forget about your popularity and seek the popularity of the Lord of the Church—that His fame might spread far and wide. The common good is your goal—not a big name, fame, and recognition for yourself.

One reason why the Israeli Air Force is the most elite in the history of the world, is because each member is after the success of the entire team, not just his own. This attitude prevails among them, and is a key reason for their success.

In 1982, over Lebanon, Israeli fighter pilots shot down eighty-seven Syrian MIG's. Not one Israeli jet pilot was shot down. Eighty-seven to zero—what a score, what a miracle, and what a team effort! I happen to know that out of every ten "would-be" jet-fighter pilots, only one goes on to become a full-fledged member in the elite ranks of fighter pilots. What of the others? Most of them become the skillful pilots of helicopter gunships. There seems to be very little strife and jealousy between the two groups, because each knows the survival of a nation rests squarely on their shoulders, and that an army divided will fall.

Another unique feature found in the Israeli Air Force is that the officer with the highest rank doesn't necessarily lead a squadron of jets into battle. If a lieutenant is the most skillful at leading a squadron into battle, and once engaged with the enemy is the most alert to changing situations, then a colonel may be placed behind him, and be quite attentive to the directions given by the lieutenant. There is no grasping for leadership in such situations, but a sober recognition of who is the most "anointed" for the job at hand.

Such should be the attitude of all of us in the Church. No one possesses all of the giftings that are unique to the Body of Christ, for God "distributes to each one individually as He wills" (1 Cor. 12:11 paraphrased).

Determine to be a team player, and allow your spiritual leaders the time to recognize the giftings God has placed in you, for their development, and your placement in God's mighty army.

4

The Enemy Kingdom

One of the things that made Jesus' ministry so unique was that He revealed the reality of Satan's kingdom in a way that had been previously unknown. Many believed in the reality of a devil, but he was a rather vague figure—hard to explain, and definitely impossible to deal with. But not so where Jesus' ministry was concerned. Jesus challenged the unseen intruder on his own turf and boldly commanded him to cease doing whatever he was busy doing in the lives of people. When Jesus came on the scene, Satan's cohorts—the demons—would cry out, and many times they would plead with Jesus not to punish them before the appointed time (Luke 8:31). The people of Jesus' day were continually amazed at this. Read what they said of Jesus' dynamic ministry of deliverance in Mark's gospel:

And they were all amazed, insomuch that they questioned among themselves, saying What thing is this?

What new doctrine is this? For with authority commandeth He even the unclean spirits, and they do obey Him. (Mark 1:27)

What's amazing is that after nineteen centuries many are still calling it *a new thing*. As Jesus continues to perform the miracle of deliverance, through His body, the Church, many will be amazed. Many will not understand, and will accuse the rising number of deliverance practitioners of "having gone overboard" in religious mania—or worse than that, they will accuse them of being possessed of the devil himself. But Jesus warned us that this would be so:

If they have called the master of the house Beelzebub, how much more shall they call them of his household? (Matt. 10:25b)

If you're going to be a member of God's end-time commando forces, you may as well get used to being misunderstood, and forget about having a good reputation with the world. Just go ahead and obey Jesus. It's so much better.

One night several years ago at our church in Monterey, a woman and her husband came forward after the meeting to be filled with the Holy Spirit. I laid my left hand gently on the lady's head and laid my right hand gently on the man's head. They were both baptized in the Holy Spirit and began to pray in unknown tongues as the Spirit gave them utterance.

As I stood before them, with my hands still on their heads, and continued praying over them, the woman fell under the power of the Holy Spirit. I can remember glancing down at her and seeing the heavenly smile on her face, and then telling her alarmed husband not to fear, that being slain in the Spirit was a common occurance. I continued praying for him for a few more minutes and then released him to return to his seat. When I looked down at the woman again, I noticed that a big change in her countenance had taken place. Instead of the heavenly smile, the expression was one of demonic torment. Her eyes and mouth were tightly shut and her head was rocking back and forth. She was moaning deeply and I could tell that she was unable to open her eyes. I immediately heard the voice of the Lord saying, *"Cast that thing out of her!"*

I dropped to my knees beside her and started commanding the demon to loose her and come out in Jesus' name! Almost instantly she jumped to her hands and knees and started attacking me like a wild animal. Her eyes remained tightly shut but her mouth was open wide, and she was snarling and growling like a rabid dog. One of the church elders and the woman's husband jumped on her to hold her down and keep her away from me. It was all they could do to hold her back in spite of the fact that they both outweighed her significantly. She was trying to bite me and scratch my eyes out. She also tried to kill herself by banging her head on the corner of a speaker cabinet and on the floor.

I simply kept yelling out, "Come out of her, you foul demon, in the name of Jesus Christ of Nazareth!" Finally, after a battle that lasted about five minutes, the tormentor came out of her with the loudest, most blood-curdling scream I have ever heard. The woman collapsed on the floor and appeared to be dead, but I knew this was not the case. The spiritual battle had totally exhausted her physical body.

I gently took her by the hand, telling her that Jesus had set her free. That heavenly smile returned to her face as life flowed back into her body. She rose to a sitting position and began to worship Jesus in spirit and in truth.

The Lord told me, that in her case, it took the powerful entrance of His Spirit in baptism to bring that strong evil spirit to the surface where I could deal with it. When the Holy Spirit came upon her in such a mighty way, He acted as one who stirs up a hornets nest by using a long stick. It greatly maddened that demon spirit.

Without going into any further graphic details, we had to cast out two or three additional demons from her that night. Suffice it to say, each one put on the same show that the first one had.

There may have been people there that night who might have misunderstood what was happening. People passing by on the street that night could have heard her screams as the demons left her. When you follow Jesus' patterns of ministry, you are going to run the risk of being totally misunderstood and totally misrepresented. But don't fret. When you came to Jesus, and vowed to serve and follow Him wherever He would lead you, you gave up your right to a good reputation. It matters not what men will say about you, as long as you are acting in accord with God's instructions.

In order for you to be a success at liberating captives from the clutches of Satan's prisons, you're going to have to have a pretty good understanding of the lay-out of his kingdom. No crack commando sets out to plunder an enemy fortress without first acquiring a thorough knowledge of it's lay-out and chief personnel.

At the head of this evil kingdom, of course, is Satan himself. And make no mistake about it, he is worse than you've ever dreamed possible. He delights in influencing an entire country (America) into performing more than 1,500,000 abortions a year. He gets much joy in watching unborn babies ripped apart in their mothers' wombs. He really gets his kicks out of child pornography. He hates mankind perfectly, and he makes no bones about it. And know this: his enthusiasm for destruction is multiplied millions of times throughout his ranks of demons.

We are warring against a very complex kingdom. We are warring against a very hateful and hurtful kingdom that is bent on our destruction. No holds are barred in this "wrestling match"—anything goes.

The clear and most vivid picture of Satan's kingdom given to us in the Word of God is found in the letter of Paul to the Ephesians:

For we wrestle not against flesh and blood, but against principalities, against powers, against the rulers of the darkness of this world, against spiritual wickedness in high places.

For a more literal rendering of this verse from the Scriptures, I will use an amplification of it from a Greek scholar who is also a spiritual warfare expert: Derek Prince. This is what I like to call *Ephesians 6:12 from the Prince Version*. (Adapted from Derek Prince's teaching at Hurlach Castle, Germany, in 1979).

Our wrestling match is not against mere human beings—people with physical bodies—but against a system of rulers with various areas of authority and with descending orders of authority, against the world dominators of this present darkness, against spiritual forces of wickedness in the heavenly regions.

Can you see the complexity of the enemy kingdom? Within this one verse from the Scriptures I see four vivid expressions of Satan's system.

Satan's kingdom is a principality. Within this principality are many smaller principalities. A principality is governed by a "prince" or ruler. This metaphor describes his rank, dignity, and jurisdiction within a kingdom—Satan's kingdom!

There is only *one* kingdom of darkness, but there are many principalities, or orders of authority within it. There are "rulers" over countries, states, cities, counties, religions, denominations, ethnic groups, political parties, etc. From their assigned positions of authority, these ruling spirits seek to manipulate and, if at all possible, to dominate the affairs of men on the earth. This fact is clearly seen in the Scriptures. From their seats of authority in the atmosphere around this planet, they work tirelessly in an all-out effort to sway the many situations on earth for Satan's good. Let us look at a scriptural example:

Then said he [the angel from God] to me, "Fear not Daniel; for from the first day that you set your heart to understand, and to chasten yourself before God, your words were heard, and I am come for your words. But the prince [ruling spirit] of the kingdom of Persia withstood me for twenty one days; but lo, Michael, one of the chief princes [of God's angels], came to help me; and I remained there with the kings of Persia. (Dan. 10:12–13)

It is clear from this section of the Scriptures that somewhere between God in heaven and Daniel praying on the earth, a great angelic battle took place before the angel with the message could get through to Daniel. I believe the upper region of our earth's atmosphere was this spiritual battleground.

The angel with the message was waylaid for nigh unto twenty-one days. Michael, perhaps the mightiest of God's angels, came to knock the resistance out of the way. Michael is the mighty angelic prince who stands for the nation of Israel (Dan. 12:1). The fact that Michael and the withstanding evil angel are both referred to as "prince" tells me that the spirits ruling in heavenly regions on Satan's behalf are indeed fallen angels. I don't believe a mere demon spirit could withstand an angel of God. I am of the firm opinion that fallen angels and demon spirits are two different classes of spiritual beings.

Angels, fallen or not, were created by God to inhabit the heavens. For an angel to indwell a human being, or an animal (Mark 5:12), would be far beneath his dignity! This would be a much lower form of existence than that for which he was created. For any angel to experience his full range of expression, he must inhabit what he was created to inhabit—the heavens.

Demons, on the other hand, crave physical bodies. They consider the body of the person they indwell as their house (Luke 11:24). Rather than being without a physical body, they are content to dwell in animals (Mark 5:12). Of course they prefer human beings over swine, but a pig beats walking through dry places, finding no rest.

A demon spirit needs someone's body in order to have a full range of expression. A demon can't rob a bank, but a demon in a man can cause the man to do so. A demon cannot rape a child, but that foul spirit, dominating from within can cause a perverted man to do so.

Demon spirits are basically filthy and moronic. The advantage they hold over mankind is one of experience. They have been at their dirty work for a long time, so they know man's weaknesses. They are familiar with his potential problem areas and each new generation of mankind is vulnerable to the time-honored tricks, strategies, and deceits of the enemy kingdom. This is precisely why we stress the necessity of getting the Word of God into people even when they are mere children. A firm knowledge of the Bible is the only basis for our freedom from vulnerability. In it we learn that we are redeemed, sanctified, and legally free from Satan's bondages. The Word lays bare his methods and goals, and Paul tells us that "we are not ignorant of his devices" (2 Cor. 2:11b). Only a firm grasp of scriptural truth, and a strong walk in the Spirit of God will remove our ignorance. If we do not have a heart knowledge of who we are in Jesus Christ, these foul demonic spirits will walk all over us.

Whether demon spirits are fallen angels or some other kind of spiritual being is really not all that important. The important thing is that we are absolute masters over them all by virtue of Jesus' victory and our identification with Him. No matter where we find them—in the heavenly regions about this planet or stalking the earth—we have God-given power over them! Actually, the name of Jesus carries certain authority in three regions: in heaven, on earth, and under the earth (Phil. 2:9–11). This is an essential truth that must be known before one can successfully assault Satan's strongholds.

In the atmosphere above this planet Satan has set the headquarters to his rival kingdom in opposition to God. He is unable to position it in the heaven of God's abode because he was expelled from it. He has done the best he can do in setting up his operation center in the heavenlies about this earth. It is not God's heaven, but it sure does beat hell. Don't be so naive as to think Satan's headquarters are in hell. He desires to incarcerate people there when they die, but he does not want to be there himself!

Hell is a place of torment, even for Satan. So he and the "pentagon" for his kingdom, are established in the heavens.

It is from this position that he and his wisest fallen angels scheme and plot, and seek to carry out the final downfall of the entire human race on the earth. Satan wants this planet, and as long as one person remains alive, his claim to it is challenged.

The officers in this rival kingdom are none other than the choice fallen angels who fell with their leader—Satan (once called Lucifer)—in rebellion against God. Beneath them in authority are other less powerful fallen angels who operate in descending orders of authority. Still lower, carrying out the "dirty work" in Satan's army, are the vile, unclean spirits—

the demons—who seek to live in human bodies and influence them to do things that are a shame even to mention.

From his headquarters in heavenly regions about this planet, Satan seeks to influence men on earth to do his will.

And Satan stood up against Israel, and provoked David to number Israel. (1 Chron. 21:1)

Satan influenced King David to do something that was wrong, something God had not told him to do. I am sure David had no idea that Satan was the one behind the thought that came to his mind that day. He probably thought it was a pretty good idea—but it was a thought from Satan.

Satan's kingdom works the same way today. He is a deceiver, and unless you know what God has already said, and have an ongoing fellowship with Him, you too can be "provoked" to do something that will help Satan's purposes.

Again, we are in warfare against principalities, or a system of rulers with various areas of authority, and descending orders of authority, against world dominators of this present darkness, against spiritual forces of wickedness in the heavenly regions.

The leaders of the communist ideology are mere pawns in Satan's hands. The leaders of the various anti-Christian cults are pawns in his hands too.

He even seeks to make good men pawns in his evil hands, as he did with King David of Israel.

As elite commando warriors, we've been given the special job of praying for our leaders. We are to pray for leaders of our country, families, and churches. As Christians, we have been given the spiritual power to "bind on earth, and bind in heaven" (Matt. 16:19). The influence of the enemy must be removed from our leaders. Therefore, we must venture into the gaps and make up the hedge for our countries, and churches, and so on. Stand fast in this day of battle (Ezek. 13:5, 22:30).

I am sure you can agree that the enemy kingdom, against which we are to wrestle, is much more complex than many would have guessed. Oftentimes there are ruling spirits over certain situations that must be taken care of before people can be freed from their bondage. These spirits are called "strongmen" by the Lord. Such evil, ruling spirits have the captive well in hand, and they must be compelled to loosen their grip before we can successfully set the captive free.

How can we do this? With weapons from God, weapons that are mighty, to the pulling down of strongholds (2 Cor. 10:4–5). And I might add, weapons that are mighty to the pulling down of "strongmen."

We deal with them with the tool of "binding and loosing" (Matt. 16:19). Our commander, the Lord Jesus, said:

> How can one enter into a strongman's house, and spoil his goods, except he first *bind* the strongman? And then he will spoil his house. (Matt. 12:29, italics mine)

This is God's strategy for dealing with Satan and his strong men. If we fail to follow Jesus' instruction, we will fail. The strong man's goods are his captives. We endeavor to enter in and plunder these goods. We are to go behind the enemy lines and set the captives free. But *first*—we must *bind* the strong man! Then *we will* spoil his goods (set the captives free).

Countless missionaries to impoverished third-world countries have failed to heed Jesus' instruction, and have died prematurely or have returned home as miserable failures. Satan and his evil spirits reign supreme in some of those dark and spiritually dead countries. The power of voodoo is rampant and witch doctors are notorious for putting curses on servants of God who seek to come in and free people from their diabolical influence. Many a sincere missionary has died a strange, agonizing death because of such a curse. The power behind the curse is an evil spirit, and usually he goes undetected.

Not long ago, my wife and I were part of a short-term missionary team ministering in Uganda, East Africa. Prior to entering, we bound the "strong man" over that country. As we encountered different situations within the boundaries of Uganda, we were diligent to bind the strong man involved, and bind all demon spirits anywhere around us. We went through many police and military roadchecks unhindered because of the success that comes from binding the enemy. Many other visitors to that country were harrassed and treated disgracefully because they did not know the authority available to them in Jesus' Name. Jesus has told us:

> Behold, I give unto you authority to tread on serpents and scorpions, and over *all* the ability of the enemy, and nothing shall *by any means* hurt you. (Luke 10:19)

But you must enforce that authority. It is not a passive authority. It must be taken up and used with diligence!

While teaching 200 pastors and evangelists in a course on spiritual warfare at Makerere College in Kampala, I asked the Lord to reveal to me the strong man over their country. I felt strongly impressed that "Islam" was his name and his aim was to make Uganda a totally Islamic country.

In Jesus' mighty name we came against him together on that day, binding him and demanding that he come down from his stolen position of authority. I encouraged the ministers of the gospel who were in my class that day to continue mercilessly assaulting his illegal position, and to continue calling forth the Lordship of Jesus Christ over their country. The future of that country is in their hands.

The anti-Christ spirit of Islam has been the chief cause of all the turmoil in that country. The poor economy, the disease, the political unrest, the terrorism, and all the rest, are the results of Islam's illegal rule over that country. Christians who know who they are in Christ can change it all.

Obviously, these are not mere ideas that I am writing about. Satan's kingdom is a very real and violent one that can only be dealt with through spiritual means.

Another example I would like to share comes from an experience I had in 1979. I was a farmer, and I came in for lunch to read our county's weekly newspaper. I was almost knocked out of my chair when I read an ad for a group of adherents to the Bahai faith. They had moved into our county, had begun "converting" people to their diabolical beliefs, and were formally setting up shop. I was appalled! Righteous indignation swept over me and I determined to do something about it—in the spiritual realm! That night I went down along the deserted country road that runs in front of our house and began to pray. I prayed in the spirit in order to tap into the wisdom of God on exactly how to deal with the situation. After an hour or so, God put it in my heart to mercilessly assault the intruding anti-Christ of Bahaism with the Name of Jesus Christ! I also slammed the Word of God into him for the killing blow! And then God let me see it. Off to my left, somewhere in the field to the east of where I was standing, a brilliant falling star (meteorite) flashed down from its way in the heavenlies and crashed into the earth. I had never seen such a display in my life. It was as though someone had ignited a sparkler and waved it in front of my face. It was indescribably brilliant! And it all happened so fast.

The Lord spoke up at that time and told me that just as surely as that meteorite had plummeted to the earth, so had the intruding spirit of anti-Christ called Bahaism when I used the authority of the Name of Jesus Christ of Nazareth against him.

Since then the Bahai movement in our county has dwindled away to almost nothing and it is a big joke in the eyes of our community. You see, we won't let it stay. We say that Jesus is Lord over our county. We'll not allow the kingdom of darkness to take any more from us than it has already taken, and we are taking back ground that was previously lost.

The Body of Christ must rise up in this hour of human history and take spiritual warfare seriously. There are imposing satanic "strong men" ruling in very many situations. These are going to have to be compelled to loosen their grip before the Body of Christ can truly take control.

God is looking for those tried men and women who will take the fight to the enemy and make war "with mighty power, to help the King against him" (2 Chron. 26:13).

As complex as the rival kingdom is, and as numerous as its members seem to be, we who make up the army of God upon the earth have nothing to fear "for there are more with us than there are with them" (2 Kings 6:16). It does not matter that within the rank and file of Satan's kingdom there are myriads of demons sent out against us. The conclusion of the Book reveals that we win! Satan, with all his angels and demons, and all the people on earth he uses so efficiently are destined to come to nothing. The New English Bible aptly puts it this way:

Its governing powers which are declining to their end. (1 Cor. 2:8)

On the other hand, we read, "Of the *increase* of Jesus' kingdom, there shall be no end" (Isa. 9:7). We are growing and expanding, and Satan and his whole lousy system are declining! Daniel recorded that God's eternal Kingdom will "never be destroyed, nor shall its sovereignty be left to another people, but it shall break, crush, and consume all these kingdoms and it shall stand *forever!*" (Dan. 2:44 TAB). This is what Satan is up against—and we are a big part of it. We are formidable in that we evoke apprehension within his ranks. He knows we are likely to be hard to deal with. We give Satan cause for fear and alarm.

We are versatile as a Kingdom people because we wield such a diversity of talents and he is unable to keep us from change. Staleness and deadness does not suit us and so Satan cannot always guess our next move. We are led by God's Spirit.

We are immeasurable in that we cannot be measured by this world's yard stick and so will not fit this world's patterns.

We are indefatigable in that we *will not* be rendered less violent with time, but as we draw ever closer in communion with God, we are made more warlike in our dealings with Satan. He really has his hands full with the "elite" of God!

Here is something else that is interesting to know about the makeup of Satan's kingdom. It compares very well to an earthly kingdom in this respect. Among his troops, Satan has guerilla spirits who make small and destructive raids that are designed to catch the enemy off guard. In his book *Angels on Assignment,* Pastor Roland Buck shared that these guerilla bands are often ambushed by a regiment of mighty angels who are sent from God to protect us. Often we know nothing of the terror that was heading our way. Psalm 91 tells us, "Thou shalt not be afraid for the terror by night; nor for the arrow that flieth by day; nor the pestilence that walks in darkness; nor for the destruction that wasteth at noonday. . . . He shall give His angels charge over thee."

How many times have we all retired for the night not knowing what evil had been lurking around the corner during the day? And we never find out because the "angel of the Lord encamps around them that reverence God, and delivers them" (Ps. 34:7).

Satan has snipers—those who shoot harmful weapons from a hidden position at individuals of its enemy force. Know this—if you are a serious Christian, you are a marked person. Keep the shield of faith held high so that you can quench all the fiery darts the sniper sends your way.

Satan employs terrorists to intimidate, and if possible to subjugate his foes. Such is a band of terrorist demons who influence men to make obscene phone calls and strike fear into the hearts of women. They terrorize people and bring them into tormenting bondage with great cunning and glee.

The kingdom of darkness has its share of spies who are sent to keep an eye on what we are doing. They closely and secretly watch and listen to us with an unfriendly purpose. I am convinced that this is why God doesn't tell us everything we would like to know. Much of what God is doing is kept secret, even from us, because He knows we would probably betray it with our words and a spy demon would carry the news to Satan. David said, "I will keep my mouth with a bridle while the wicked is before me" (Ps. 39:1b). My paraphrase takes it a bit further: "I will keep my mouth with a bridle because you never know who may be listening."

Knowing that Satan wants to divide the Body of Christ, and thereby conquer us, is it any wonder he positions his spies here and there in order to catch us in thoughtless conversations? Every time you "bad mouth" your sister or your brother, you stand the chance that "a bird of the air will go tell the matter" (Eccles. 10:20), and that feelings may be forever damaged. James wrote that if a man could not bridle his tongue, his religion was vain (Greek transliteration: "void of result"). Possess the tongue of the wise, my friend. "Be swift to hear, and slow to speak" (James 1:19).

51

There are propaganda spirits working to ruin our reputations. They will tell lies on you whether you have done anything or not, but woe unto the Christian whose bad reputation is based on truth. The Word says for us to keep ourselves pure and unspotted by the world, telling us to "avoid even the appearance of evil" (1 Thess. 5:22). Why? Because he who coined the word "propaganda" is looking for even the smallest thing to use against us. He is the "accuser of the brethren" (Rev. 12:10), and he is out to malign your name before men. But if you are guiltless, stand assured in the fact that "every tongue that rises against you, shall be shown to be in the wrong" (Isa. 54:17 TAB). God has ways to vindicate His saints.

Now let us go on and examine a few of the many pitfalls Satan places before the Christian who is intent upon assaulting his kingdom. They are varied, and there are many of them to examine. The next chapter reveals the nature of these pitfalls.

5

Enemy Pitfalls

As an effective member of God's kingdom commandos on earth you will have to know and be quick to recognize the various pitfalls the enemy will place before you.

A pitfall is a concealed trap, cleverly placed for an unwary person to fall into. If you are in one of the devil's pitfalls, you're posing no real threat to him.

Satan has set many time-proven pitfalls for ensnaring the Christian. Our list can in no way be exhaustive; however, we will reveal a few of his most successful ones. Often, these are very subtle.

Paul tells us that we should not be "ignorant of his devices" (2 Cor. 2:11), so there is nothing wrong with studying to understand the ways of the enemy. We are also told to stand against "the wiles of the devil" (Eph. 6:11), so in order to stand against something, we must of necessity know what it is. A wile is a cunningly devised plan, drawn up by Satan for your destruction. Pitfalls are a major part of that plan, and we need to become aware of them.

Through the years I have run into many sincere Christians who believe that to study such things gives too much recognition to Satan. This is not so. You study to save your neck, and the necks of countless others, because *you* are kept free of Satan's pitfalls. A free man is one who is able to lower a rope to a man in the pit. Remember that! Ignoring the devil will not make him go away, but will in fact liberate him to do more destructive things in your life. Don't be so naive as to think your safety is all up to God and that you can just lie back and lead a life of ease and luxury. God has given you the armor and He has told you to stand against the "wiles, strategies, and deceits of the wicked one" (Eph. 6:11 TAB). And another thing: do not be one who thinks that all you have to do is keep your eyes on Jesus and all your enemies will go away. It just doesn't work that way—your enemy will have a heyday in your life if that is your approach.

The best defense is a good offense, and as we become "headhunters for God," looking to decapitate our spiritual foes as David did Goliath, the giant of Gath, we will become adept at overthrowing the imposing works of hell, and setting the captives free.

God is calling for a larger, faster, and stronger army in this last hour of human history (as we know it). No one disbands a fire department to stop fires, no one disbands a police department to stop crime, and if we disarm and disband the people of God and call on them to be spiritually passive, we will not stop Satan's kingdom from taking advantage of us. Satan interprets our passivity as a weakness to be exploited, a doormat to be trod upon. George Washington said, "If we desire to avoid insult as a country, we must be ready to repel it; if we desire to secure peace . . . it must be known that we are at all times ready for war!" I wish my passive brothers and sisters would permit this reality to be burned into their thinking.

Years ago, and long before I became a Christian, there was a bully in the school I attended who took great delight in beating up on me. He was four or five inches taller than I

54

was, and he outweighed me by at least fifty pounds. I was a total pushover and he knew it. I did every passive thing I could think of in order to avoid conflict with him, but nothing ever helped; he always hunted me down. He persisted for a period of months—punching me, shoving me around, verbally insulting me, and embarrassing me in front of all my classmates.

One day I took my concern to my dad, hoping that he could give me some helpful advice. As I related my story to him, he was greatly troubled. No father in his right mind likes to hear of his own flesh-and-blood son being bullied and shamed by an overbearing schoolyard bully. Though dad's advice was radical and is probably not the advice you would feel free to give to your son, it sets forth the principle we have been looking at concerning the proper repulsion of an aggressor. Dad told me to wait until the next time the bully started in on me. He said that I should turn as though I was going to walk away from him, and then suddenly wheel around and hit him on the top of his nose as hard as I could. He told me that this would stagger him—bringing forth blood from his nose, tears from his eyes, and temporary and partial blindness. I was then to get the bully down on the ground and "kick the stuffings out of him." In this weakened state, from the punch on the nose, I would be able to do this effectively. Dad said that if I punched him on the nose, but failed to follow through with it by giving him a sound beating, then he would probably kill me.

Although my dad's advice at that time (he has since become a Christian) could be heartily argued against, I can gladly report to you that it proved to be my deliverance from that bully. The only law he respected was force and he soon learned that I wasn't the passive, weak little puppy he thought I was. I never had any more trouble with him. Not only that, but I never had trouble with anyone else. I guess I quickly developed a reputation of being a tough guy. The potential bullies in our school respected my willingness to fight if push came to shove, and they left me alone.

I have since seen this application of force work many times over in the area of spiritual warfare. When I assault an evil spirit in the name of Jesus and with the Word of God I won't let up until I know I have whipped him soundly! Once all is done, I usually never have to face that one again.

Evil spirits, like schoolyard bullies, know who they can or cannot fool with. If you stand tall against Satan and his cohorts and show them you are going to fight for however long it takes, you won't have to fight very long. Satan knows he cannot beat the Word of God. He knows he cannot beat you if you are standing firmly on that Word. But he is convinced that, through persistence, he can get you off the Word of God. Jesus said that Satan's persecutions and afflictions come for the Word's sake (Mark 4:17). He comes to take the Word of God out of your heart and from underneath your spiritual feet. Do not let him do it! Resist the devil, and he will flee from you!

General George Marshall said, "We have tried since the birth of our nation [America] to promote our love of peace by a display of weakness. [So has the Church]. This course has cost us millions of lives and billions of treasure. The reasons are quite understandable. The world does not seriously regard the desires of the weak. Weakness presents too great a temptation to the strong. We must, if we are to realize the hopes that we may now dare for a lasting peace, reinforce our will for peace with strength. We must make it clear to the potential gangsters of the world that if they dare break our peace they will do so at their great peril!"[1] I love that mentality! But in the Church I carry it even further in that I want to force my way into enemy-occupied territory and begin liberating the masses held in bondage there. Jesus Christ set His Church *against* the work of hell! The truth of the matter is that we in Zion are not in a time of peace and tranquility, but we are at war—and it is the war of the ages! Jesus didn't send us forth in His army to lose gracefully, but He sent us forth to win—and to win decisively! We dare not sit back passively and hope it will all get better, but we must go forth in great power to bring release to this earth, and the consummation of this age.

In dealing with the various traps and pitfalls of the enemy, it will be rewarding to commit this verse of Scripture to memory:

[1] Alexander, Holmes; *Never Lose a War;* Dezin-Adair Publishing; Greenwich, Conn.;—1984

Our soul [whole being] is escaped as a bird out of the snare of the trapper; The snare is *broken* and we are escaped. (Ps. 124:7)

This is what I call a redemptive Psalm because it has to do with the great things the Lord has done for His people in redemption. It has to do with the redeeming work of Jesus Christ at Calvary. Notice that it says, "The snare is broken." The Word tells us that Jesus was manifested, that He might destroy the works of the devil (1 John 3:8b). This is precisely what took place as Jesus hung on that cross, for Paul wrote that "God disarmed the principalities and powers ranged against us" (Col. 2:15 TAB). It goes on to say that He triumphed over them for us and led, as a conquering King, a long train of captives in a victory parade; He showed off the spoils of battle! At the cross, Jesus went right through all of Satan's ranks and right into his very headquarters and stripped him of his authority. Jesus perfectly walked Satan's trapline and sprung every one of his traps. Jesus dealt the death blow to Satan, and he has been losing strength ever since.

The Body of Christ on earth is to serve as the occupation force that stays on the scene after a country has fallen. Should a revolt arise, the occupation force must be quick to squelch it and enforce its country's victory. So it is with the Church, where spiritual things are concerned.

Sadly, we have not done a good job. Not too long after Jesus ascended into heaven, the Church became very religious, allowing the devil to lull it to sleep in great false religions. The Word of God was taken out of the hands of the common people and delivered to the cult priests who Satan raised up in that hour. As the priests lied to the people by distorting the basic doctrines of the Church, the world was thrown into the Dark Ages. Satan's diabolical, *broken* trap wrapped its jaws around the Church and held it in check for several hundred years during which time Satan unleashed his fury upon the earth with barbaric wars, famines, and great pestilences.

Eventually God was able to raise up a man named Martin Luther who was unsettled in the belief that one must produce enough good works in order to merit heaven. He found that the "Just shall live by faith" (Rom. 1:17), and that to place trust in any other thing but the blood of Jesus Christ was vanity. He saw that faith in Christ's sacrifice alone was all that was necessary to put a person in right standing with God, and that by coming to God with that faith one could be cleansed of his sins in this life, and go to heaven. This smacked hard against the teaching of the day, but Luther would not back down. He had a greater fear of displeasing God than of displeasing men. From that time (early 1500s) till today, the Church has been coming more and more out of darkness. We are on a roll and we dare not stop now.

Jesus soundly whipped Satan 2,000 years ago and the snare is indeed *broken!* We must know that we go forth in Christ's authority to police and govern this planet from our spiritual position in Him (Eph. 2:6).

All over this planet there are people sitting in broken traps and they don't even know it. Many know they are enslaved, but they don't realize how easy it is to get out. Still others are so deceived that they don't even realize they have problems with a snare of the enemy. (Look at the alcoholic who doesn't think he is one). As we go to them with the truth from God's Word, the walls of deception will come tumbling down and they will go free in Jesus' Name.

My wife, Darlene, and I have taken delight in helping to rescue people from bondage. Whether this takes the form of their being headed for financial disaster or for times of sickness and disease is not the real issue. We have the Word of God and the anointing that will bring the corrections needed to get them back on the proper paths, regardless of the form of bondage.

David said, "Concerning the works of men, by the word of thy lips I have kept me from the paths of the destroyer" (Psa. 17:4).

We have been able to thwart disaster in the area of sickness and disease by ministering knowledge to people concerning proper diet, rest, and exercise. We have foreseen financial disaster coming to others and have been able to assist them in curtailing unnecessary spending, setting up a working budget, and by sharing with them sound investment opportunities.

Most folks don't even know that a better way is within their reach. What a pleasure to hand to them the answers that have set us free from so much turmoil and disaster.

Concerning finances, in the lives of one couple, we were able to give them some very basic instruction that freed them from financial problems over a period of months.

Darlene taught the wife how to shop. She had been spending large amounts of money on things she really could have done without or that she could have made much more economically at home. She helped her in shopping for groceries and cut her monthly grocery bill by better than a third.

I worked with the man, and discovered that though he was tithing regularly he was not speaking the Word of God diligently over his finances. Giving the tithe is not enough. We are to be in the habit of speaking the Word over our giving and over the finances God has entrusted to us. When he began doing this, freedom came.

As we go forth to win the lost, heal the sick, cast out demons, mend marriages, open blind eyes, and tear down strongholds, the enemy will attempt to counter our offensives by laying many cleverly devised traps and pitfalls, hoping to stop our forward progress. He has been at work for centuries and so he qualifies as no one's fool. It pays for us to go forth knowing what to expect from him.

PITFALL #1

"The cares of this world" (Mark 4:19).

One translation calls them "the responsibilities of this age." A major pitfall for you to be "coaxed" into is that of getting too busy in life's affairs—even the nice-sounding ones—and being subtly removed from the real field of battle. When you must work two jobs in order to make ends meet, you pose no threat to the enemy and his kingdom. When you allow your in-laws, aunts and uncles, cousins, etc. to manipulate all your free time, you pose no threat to the prison houses of Satan. As you pursue hobbies, fun and games in all of your "off hours," and never venture into the breach in the day of battle, or never stand fast for the lost, sick, and dying around you, you become a deplorable "joke" in the eyes of your comrades who need you. I stand amazed at the would-be "mighty men" who have allowed Satan to lull them into uselessness during this war of the ages. They are so wrapped up in the cares of this life, that they can no longer see the fray.

Jesus exhorted us to "take heed to ourselves, lest at any time our hearts become overcharged with . . . the cares of this life" (Luke 21:34). He went on to tell us to "watch and pray always that we may be accounted worthy to escape all the things that will come to pass, and to stand before Him" (Luke 21:36). I truly fear for many of my brothers and sisters who are taking a nonchalant view of the days we are living in and the ones that are fast approaching. "Perilous times" are really coming, and we had better prepare for them. Too many Christians are behaving like the foolish virgins of Matthew 25 who failed to purchase enough oil for their lamps. When the midnight hour was upon them they found their meager supply had run out, and they were rejected. The "night is far spent" and we had better "get on the ball" where spiritual things are concerned.

As the old hymn rings out:

Rise up, O men of God,
Have done with lesser things,
Give heart and soul and mind and strength,
To serve the King of kings!

PITFALL #2

Procrastination.

Between your present location and the enemy fortress over yonder there are many pitfalls of procrastination masquerading as "legitimate reasons to put off today what can be accomplished tomorrow." Putting it bluntly, this is "never doing today what you can put off indefinitely." Guys and gals of all ages are doing this throughout the Body of Christ.

It burns me to see men who could be serving in the trenches

with me, "warring a good warfare" (1 Tim. 1:18), being ruled by their "good intentions" instead. Good intentions do not win wars! Good intentions are not where the water hits the wheel in spiritual things, and in this hour we desperately need men and women of war who will put action to their good intentions.

The one who always talks of doing something, but never gets around to doing it is a very real disappointment—like clouds and wind without rain (Prov. 25:14).

I was a farmer for seventeen years, and at the time of this writing I still make a couple of thousand bales of hay each summer. I know all too well what it is to be in the midst of a drought, and see dark clouds pass overhead all day long without spilling any rain on your dry and thirsty land. Oh, what a desperate and disappointing feeling this brings. This is precisely how I feel when I look around at all the potential commandos for Jesus who are only talking and not doing.

How well do you suppose it would be accepted on the front lines of a natural war if some procrastinating soldier were to let his commanding officer down by not being where he is supposed to be when he's supposed to be there? Suppose, as a result, men died or were taken captive by the enemy? How would you feel if you were the officer in charge of those men's lives? Why, you'd feel like shooting the "ding-a-ling" if he didn't have a good excuse for his tardiness! If he were to excuse himself by saying, "Well, I meant to be there; it's just that I had some other things I wanted to do and I thought I could put it off for a while." You would feel like wringing his neck right on the spot! A procrastinator costs men their lives. This holds true in the area of spiritual warfare too.

There are folks who will die and go to hell because you don't pray. Others will die prematurely because you put off going to them with the Word of God on healing and health. There are couples who will split up in divorce because no one trained in Spirit-filled marriage counseling will go to them and help them salvage their marriage. You are thinking you would like to do these things sometime, but you are not getting around to doing them now. How shameful! Freely you have received, freely give. Beware of those subtle holes of procrastination. They lie everywhere before you, and you must conquer them.

PITFALL #3

Expecting God to do it all for you.

I read a story in a Christian periodical about a farmer who bought a scrub piece of land for next to nothing. After much toil, he developed it into a small farm that anyone would be proud to own. It had an immaculate fruit orchard, well-defined meadows, rock-free pastures, and well-developed watering holes for his cattle. One day a friend came by to visit him, and upon seeing the beauty of the farm he commented, "You and the Lord sure have a nice farm here."

"Yes," the farmer replied, "but you should've seen it when the Lord had it all by himself!"

Actually God could have developed that ground all by himself, but He did not choose to do so. God wanted to work with the farmer by blessing the fruit of his labor. The Bible calls us "co-laborers with God" (1 Cor. 3:9).

A dangerous misunderstanding many have today is that God really doesn't need much from man because, after all, He is God! If you really examine this perverted belief you can see the lazy, freeloading bum it can produce. Many churches have allowed this mentality to slip in among the flock and rob them of their initiative. But the truth is that God won't let us off the hook, and we may as well get that straight. He is not going to win your city, or your county to the Kingdom apart from you doing your part. You need to pray, and develop your soul-winning skills. You need to be passing out tracts as much as the next man. You need to be involved in your church's spiritual warfare and intercessory prayer gatherings. God is depending on you to win those battles, and take that ground *with* Him! So whether it is your own battle, or a battle for the freedom of someone else, roll up your sleeves and dive in. As you do, you will discover that God himself is right there with you, working all things for good.

PITFALL #4

Lack of discipline in spiritual things.

Hubbard said, "God will not look you over for medals—but for scars." True spiritual scars come from intense times of battle, but there are many who shall stand scarless before Jesus at His appearing because they never trained hard to become battle-ready. God can't use them much, because they lack discipline. Discipline is a lost art in the pampered Christianity of the twentieth-century, "Americanized" Church. But God wants no pampered saints where spiritual preparation is concerned. In order to be strong in spiritual strength and exploits, one needs to be strong in spiritual discipline.

In today's turbulent world, where Satan runs roughshod over the masses, God wants disciplined men and women—tried, true, and battle-poised. Does he find such men and women as this? Too often He does not!

The plight of modern man is seen in his striving for the road of self-indulgence, and the path of least resistance. He is lazy and irresponsible when it comes to spiritual discipline because discipline is hard work and is not fun. We like fun things. Another fact about discipline is that it simply beats hard against our tendency to be "laid back" and uninvolved. We have developed a live-and-let-live attitude about everything and, besides, it's easier to stay home and lead a quiet, peaceable life. But I tell you that unless we are disciplined in spiritual practices, we can lose our freedom, and our quiet, peaceable lives can be taken from us!

The purpose of discipline is that we might expand spiritually. But as one man wrote, "Spiritual expansion can be excruciating." If you've ever lifted weights in order to increase the size of your muscles you know what this means. As you complete a set, pumping that iron those last two or three strokes—pushing or pulling for all you are worth—it feels like your muscles are going to self-destruct. The pain is excruciating.

This is what it is like to pray when you know you should, but you just don't feel like it, but you do it anyway. This excruciating feeling is what you may experience as you give financial gifts to God out of what seems to be a tremendous lack in your earthly account. But you do it because you require it of yourself and you bite the bullet for Him. Nowadays, men would rather do without spiritual exploits than to work for them. Sacrifice and self-discipline are "ideas" hard

63

to come by these days. Discipline is what the Church needs the most, and wants the least—yet, the world belongs to the disciplined.

Discipline yourself in times of prayer, knowing that many Christian endeavors fail because of lack of prayer. Discipline yourself in regular times in the Word, because this is the only thing that will keep your faith for victory, growing and strong. Discipline yourself into spending regular times of fellowship with believers of like, precious faith, knowing that one stick, standing alone, can be easily broken, but a bundle of sticks cannot. Discipline yourself into speaking the Word of God, or things that are in line with the Word of God, knowing that you can be brought into bondage by speaking wrong words (Prov. 6:2, 13:3, 18:21). Discipline yourself to do what the Word is telling you to do; be a "doer" of the Word, not a hearer only, deceiving your own self (James 1:22).

Paul said, "I keep under my body, and bring it into subjection . . . lest I be cast away" (1 Cor. 9:27). The flesh would rather watch TV tonight than pray. The flesh would rather sleep that extra hour in bed tomorrow morning, than get up and spend an hour in the Word. It is the flesh—that body—that desperately desires to stay uninvolved in spiritual disciplines. Rise up, child of God, and reign in life by Jesus Christ, telling your body what it can or cannot do!

You know there are a few precious souls who have made up their minds that they are going on in God. They, like Paul, are going "to keep under their bodies." There is a race set before them and they are determined to run it so as to win (Heb. 12:1). If you join them, everything will be fine! If you choose not to, then know this: they will not wait for you. They will run on ahead and leave you in their dust. Folks like these have set their faces like flint to go on, but what about you? Are you going to complain when you see the pastor spending more time with them than he is with you? Are you going to be jealous when you see them more in the limelight of spiritual activity than you are? No! No! No! Be one of those "elite" warriors who train hard to make things happen for God's glory.

PITFALL #5

Wrong motivation. (The wrong reason for being and doing what you are.)

What motivates you to be an elite warrior for God? Be sure you know the answer to this one.

The desire to be a big somebody—loved, wooed, and admired—often carries over into one's Christian life. Just because you got saved does not automatically remove those wrong motives and deceitful aspirations from you.

A young man who always wanted to be a famous rock star—in the limelight, and internationally known—gets saved. Before long he gives up his dream of one day becoming a big rock star, because now he wants to be a great preacher, like the one he sees on TV every Sunday. That preacher's life style appears to be so glamorous and full of good times. He is known the world over and is, in most circles, held in high esteem. This appeals to many young "preacher boys." Their main underlying motive for ministry is that they might be seen and admired of men.

On the local church level, there are those who aspire to eldership because they can't stand to be a part of something that they are not in charge of. This abominable, selfish attitude and motivation is very often a carry over from the years they spent as a part of the selfish world system.

Such ungodly motives for ministry must be dealt the death blow. If you believe God will use you when you have these hanging on you, you have some disappointing times ahead of you. You see, "God resists the proud, but gives grace to the humble" (1 Pet. 5:5).

Examine yourself my fellow-soldier, and get the idea that "the cream always rises to the top" out of your sick head. God will put you down if you think yourself the cream over your brothers and sisters. Philippians 2:3 exhorts us, "In lowliness of mind, esteem others as better than ourselves." Remember this my friend:

The lofty looks of man shall be humbled, and the haughtiness of men shall be bowed down, and the Lord alone shall be exalted in that day. For the day of the Lord of hosts shall be upon every one that is proud and lofty, and upon every one that is lifted up; and *he shall* be brought low. (Isa. 2:11–12)

All that you are, and all that you ever hope to be for God's kingdom, is only because of His unmerited favor in your life. Your motive for ministry should always be to meet the needs of people, to totally glorify God, the Father, and your Lord Jesus Christ, and to please the Holy Spirit. Seek no personal glory in anything you do, and then if you don't get it, it won't bother you.

PITFALL #6
Condemnation.
James said, "We all stumble in many ways" (James 3:2, NAS). It is what you do after you stumble and fall that counts. Many Christians lie there in the dust of condemnation, self-pity, and defeat, and Satan dances on down the street, laughing his fool head off.

You know what I do when I sin and fall? I get right back up, dust myself off, confess my sin to the Lord (I John 1:9), and shout right into the devil's condemning face, "So what's it to you, Mr. Devil? My sin is none of your cotton-pickin' business!" And you know, it isn't. He's not my lord. He can condemn me all he wants, but I'll not pay him any attention because through confession of that sin I am washed in the purifying blood of Jesus!

So what if the devil condemns you? Does that mean God does too? God forbid that He should ever do something because Satan does it. God is so far above Satan (and so are you) that it's comical. The scripture says:

Who shall lay anything to the charge of God's elect? It is God that justifies. Who is he that condemns? It is Christ that died, yes, rather, that is risen again, who is even at the right hand of God, who also makes intercession for us. (Rom. 8:33–34)

Praise God, Jesus is praying for us—not condemning us! Satan is the condemner; God is the justifier. As you confess the sin, and renounce it in your life, the precious blood of Jesus purifies you and God justifies you.

Yet, so many Christians allow Satan's broken trap of condemnation to keep them in bondage. This ought not to be!

Get up when you fall. The Bible says that the righteous man falls seven times, but gets up again and again (Prov. 24:16). Larry Tomczak said, "Champions don't give up, they get up!" That's who you are if you belong to Jesus—a champion!

Nothing you have done, or ever dreamed of doing can separate you from the love of God, which is in Christ Jesus our Lord (Rom. 8:39). The time is at hand to lean hard on His forgiveness and His mercy. He will abundantly pardon. Exert faith in that, and tell Satan and his unfounded condemnation to "hit the road, Jack!"

PITFALL #7

Self-debasement.

While it is true that we are "in lowliness of mind," "to esteem others better than ourselves," we are in no way to debase ourselves. Lowliness of mind does not mean self-debasement.

Paul said we are to "think soberly," not more highly of ourselves than we ought to think, but *soberly*—as God has dealt to us a measure of faith (Rom. 12:3).

A sober evaluation of oneself is healthy. I know that apart from the grace of God in my life I am a nothing, and that without faith I cannot be a God-pleaser. I know that without open lines of communication with God, I'm a disaster going somewhere to happen. But, *praise God!* I am not without God's grace, and I am not without faith, because He has dealt to me a measure, and it's increasing. I am not without open lines of communication with Him.

In His Word I see that He has made me "more than a conqueror" (Rom. 8:37). I see in His word that I can "be strong in the Lord, and in the power of His might" (Eph. 6:10).

No longer debase yourself. Stop considering yourself to be a worm in the dust—filthy, repulsive, and of no earthly use to anyone.

You are a child of the most high God! You have great potential, and God chose you from before the forming of the world. You are the clay, and He is the potter who can mold you, and has molded you into His creative masterpiece.

Stop siding in with "Old Slewfoot" and downgrading yourself! You are precious in His sight. He hasn't given up on you yet, so why should you?

PITFALL #8
Strife.

This is a big pitfall. Volumes have already been written concerning the dangers of strife, unforgiveness, criticism, and resentment. If you get pinned down in the barbed-wire entanglements of strife, you become "a sittin' duck" for the enemy. He'll blast away at you from his machine-gun nest on the hill.

The most subtle entanglements of Satan are often found within the realm of interpersonal relationships. He attempts to ensnare you with strife in the family. He wants husbands and wives bickering and threatening divorce. He desires to turn the hearts of the fathers and sons against one another because he knows that this will provoke a curse, and further desolation within the confines of this world (Mal. 4:6).

If you make it through this entanglement, then he will seek to bog you down in strife within the local church. In either entanglement, you pose no threat to his prison houses. The hostages will remain hostages, because of your entrapment in strife.

1 Corinthians 13 teaches that strife jerks the rug out from under the gifts of the Spirit in one's life. If you pray in tongues of men and of angels, and have not love . . . you are nothing. Strife is the opposite of love.

The problem I had with strife and bitterness was another thing I had to overcome after becoming a Christian. All of my life I had been around people who were full of strife and its bitterness. The strife that possessed us was often mani-

68

fested through malicious backbiting and critical gossip. I was well-trained in this damaging art and I could verbally roll-to-pieces anyone with whom I had a grievance.

Not long after becoming a Christian I began to see that this was wrong. The Scriptures abound with verses which condemn strife in its different forms. However, knowing what God expects from me and performing it to His pleasure are two different things. During my first few years as a Christian I continued on in the deplorable sin of strife. I knew it was dead wrong and I abhorred the fact that I was under its control. I would sin and repent, sin and repent, but never did I find lasting victory, until the day I heard a preacher on a cassette tape relate how he had gained victory over gluttony by putting a bit in his mouth. This made me curious. What did he mean when he said he put a bit in his mouth? As I continued to listen, he related how he had drawn up a formal contract between himself and the Lord, stating that he would not be controlled by his unruly appetite anymore, but would, with God as his helper, begin to control his appetite and bring it into subjection to his spirit. He dated it, had his wife sign it along with his children, and began that day to reign over his belly by Jesus Christ.

By the act of signing and dating that written declaration in the presence of his family, and by having them sign their names to it as his witnesses, he bound himself to that oath and thus, put a bit in his mouth. No longer was he free to turn to the right or the left, because that bit held him to the straight and narrow. Needless to say, he won his battle. There is power in putting your name to something in the presence of witnesses.

After I heard this remarkable story I went into my study and typed up a "bit" to be placed in my mouth. It read as follows:

I, Chip Hill, being of sound mind, do hereby, on this twenty-fifth day of September, 1977, vow to put an end to the longstanding habit of criticizing others behind their backs. With the Holy Spirit as my helper and standby, I refuse to lend my tongue to the spreading of malicious lies and defaming reports. I will speak only that which is good to the use of edifying, that it may minister grace to all hearers. All bitterness, wrath,

anger, strife, and evil speaking is this day put far from
me for the glory of God. I bind myself to this oath.

Chip Hill

I also had my wife sign her name to it, and then I taped it
to our refrigerator door so as to be constantly reminded of
it. Within six months time, the strong back of strife and
criticism was soundly broken.

My ministry seemed to take off after strife was dealt with
and God began to use me in greater ways than ever before.

Beware of the ever-present pitfall of strife and discord
within home and church.

PITFALL #9

Storming ahead without enough prayer.

We've all been guilty of this one! We are to do everything by
prayer, and nothing without it (Phil. 4:6). Jesus said men ought
always to pray, and not faint. I tell you, that unless Christian
action is birthed in prayer, upheld in prayer, maintained by
prayer, and finished in prayer, it will likely fail.

I have learned that when I am lulled into the pitfall of
prayerlessness I become highly ineffective in walking in the
power of God. Things that would not normally cause me to
stumble and faint become as giants before me.

The only remedy I have found for the life of prayerlessness is in what the Scriptures say David did in one of his
times of trouble. He "encouraged himself in the Lord his
God" (1 Sam. 30:6).

There comes the time when you must grit your teeth and
pull yourself up by your own bootstraps. There is only one
remedy for prayerlessness, and that is prayer! How many
times have I forced myself to my prayer closet in order to
commune formally with God? Too many to remember. But
in each case I can honestly say that I have emerged from my
closet in much better spiritual and mental condition than
when I first went in.

Prayer keeps things in perspective and keeps your spirit
in fine tune with the signals God sends you by His Spirit.
Prayer makes the difference in whether you succeed in ministry or fail.

There are so many would-be commandos for Jesus who are falling by the multitudes because they have failed to be men of prayer first. It is in the prayer closet where you receive the true baptism of power. Victorious Christian endeavor can only be carried on from the prayer closet. Examine closely the prayer life of our Commander Jesus Christ. He was so successful among the people because He was so mighty in prayer! We can be no different. Make sure you are a praying commando.

PITFALL #10

Departure from the simplicity of the gospel.

Satan is a past master at drawing us away from the simple gospel message. He hates the simple gospel for it is the power of God that saves (Rom. 1:16). You and I know that God chose to save us "through the foolishness of preaching" (1 Cor. 1:21). Preaching in itself doesn't do it, but it's what we preach to our neighbors and friends that does the job. We can present nothing but the simple gospel message as we find it in the written Word of God.

Intellectual hodgepodge will not do it. The great apostle knew this well and he was the one who said, "For I determined [he had to determine this] not to know anything among you, save Jesus Christ, and Him crucified" (1Cor. 2:2). Intellectually he could have blown their minds, but it would have done them no good. Paul was also the one who said, "But I fear, lest by any means, as the serpent beguiled Eve through his subtilty, so your minds should be corrupted from the simplicity that is in Christ (2 Cor. 11:3). By the means of vain philosophy, human reason and logic, humanistic teaching, and the cultist's lie, we find men who have strayed from the simple teaching of the Word of God, and who preach another Jesus, present another gospel, and deliver another spirit to the masses of dying humanity. Oh, that God would raise up His mighty end-time army to go forth in this hour and set the record straight! "And this is the record, that God has given us eternal life, and this life is in His Son. He that has the Son has life; and he that has not the Son of God has not life" (1 John 5:11–12). It is so pure and simple. Never allow yourself to be deceived into presenting any other gospel. The gospel we are to preach is one that the common man can grab and run with. Never allow yourself to be involved with a gospel that has "a form of godliness, but that denies the power thereof" (2 Tim. 3:5). If the true gospel is being presented, its power will change lives (Jer. 23:22).

My fellow-commando, I have taken the time to show you just a few of the many time-proven pitfalls of the enemy. Go forward with your head up, and your eyes attentive to what lies before you. Remember this: Jesus will not ask you to go anywhere unless He has first walked there himself. He knows all the pitfalls. He knows their whereabouts, and exactly how to avoid them. Cling to Him and He will see you safely through them all.

6

Lines of Communication

I did not include this chapter in my original manuscript. But because of recent events in our church I felt the urging of the Lord to include it now. This business of communication is so important, and if we fail here, we are liable to see all our work for God come tumbling down.

The problem I had to face as I emerged into the role of pastor in my home church in Monterey, Virginia, was that of becoming recognized as someone other than "just one of the boys." When our "flow" began in January of 1978, I was a full-time farmer, raising beef cattle and sheep. I began a small Bible study in our home, and I taught the authority of the Word of God with youthful zeal. The Lord began to send people to us who were hungering and thirsting after the things of God. Folks were saved, healed, delivered, baptized with the Holy Spirit, and "super-charged" with the Word of God. For a period of twenty-two exciting months this continued, until in

November of 1979, God showed us that it was time to "close down shop." That didn't make a whole lot of sense to us. After all, our house was packed out every Tuesday night as the Lord was bringing people from even the next county for ministry. We were a success, and you don't shift gears, or change directions when everything is going well—right? Don't count on it. God is God, and He is all-wise, and sovereign. We simply obeyed. For a whole year we had nothing. No ministry, no teaching, not anything. At the outset of this year, just after we had canceled all further meetings, God had spoken to me and said, *"Phase one of what I am doing in Highland County is coming to an end. Phase two will begin, and it will dwarf phase one in size and scope."*

I responded, "Okay, Lord," and expected to see phase two begin immediately, but nothing happened, and I was not supposed to try and make things happen either. At this same time, Larry Whetzel, who is now a pastor in our Monterey church, had a spiritual vision in which he saw our fledgling church standing before God as a mere babe—in stark nakedness. In this vision the Lord showed him that we had been stripped of our diapers, and were standing naked before Him, awaiting our training pants. As he shared this vision with me, we saw that we were totally dependent on God to put us in our training pants, and all we could do in the meantime was wait and pray.

Approximately one year later God, in His infinite wisdom, put us into our training pants. We were instructed to rent an old Ford garage that was in the process of being remodeled, and was situated right in the middle of Monterey—the county seat. As we slipped into our training pants (the start of phase two) we found that we were perfectly central to the whole county of Highland. In the years that ensued the Lord sent a stream of people our way. We became the big talk of the town (not all of it was good), and passed milestone after milestone in our growth to maturity. On the surface if appeared as though everything was going great, but deep beneath the ground, where the foundation was built, there was serious trouble.

All of this was built up around a man whose aspiration was to be a good Bible teacher, and that's all. I, for the life of me, couldn't see myself as a pastor. My opinion of pastors was somewhat immature—I thought they were all sissy fellows—after all, that's all I ever saw as I grew up. But as the Lord reeducated me to the truth, I began, ever so slowly, to embrace the true call he had placed on my life. In time I was recognized as the "pastor," and yet there were those people who deep down still considered me as just one of the boys. This made it hard to lead them, as they weren't wholly committed to trust and follow my leading. I have since learned, and I am instilling this principle into the flock, that there comes a time when a leader's relationship to his followers must shift somewhat in order for him to be the best leader he can be. This principle is clearly seen in the way Jesus began to treat His own family and friends soon after He began the public phase of His ministry.

> And on the third day there was a wedding in Cana of Galilee; and the mother of Jesus was there; and Jesus also was invited, and His disciples, to the wedding. And when the wine gave out, the mother of Jesus said to Him, "They have no wine." And Jesus said to her, "Woman, what do I have to do with you? My hour has not yet come."

Jesus' rebuke of His own mother may seem a bit hard for us to understand, but it was just that Mary had to learn that her relationship with Jesus was going to change. Highly favored though Mary was, she had to learn that in matters affecting His ministry, He could only move at His Father's bidding, and that their special human relationship must now fade into the background. This lesson is reinforced in Mark's gospel, chapter three, verses 31–35. In these verses we find the claims of His family set against the claims of His ministry. We see Jesus giving priority to the spiritual relationship over against the natural.

This is precisely what I have had to do in Monterey, and I have had to run the risk that some people's feelings might get hurt. It has not been easy, but I can honestly say that folks are coming around. You see, it all began wrong in Monterey, because in our ignorance, we built a faulty foundation. We are not making that mistake in the other churches we have started; we learned some hard lessons in Monterey. I praise God that His people there have been so patient and teachable.

The second problem with our foundation in Monterey was that from our beginnings we did not stress the importance of open and immediate communication among our members. As Americans, we had adopted the philosophy that it's best to sweep problems between us under the rug, and try to behave as though nothing was ever wrong. That all sounds nice, but it simply doesn't work. We have the tendency to avoid conflict at all cost, and this has cost the church in America dearly.

In Monterey there were little grievances among certain members that were never resolved, and so over the period of six or seven years were allowed to lie hidden as they festered and eventually erupted into attitudes that were very ugly and potentially destructive. Had it not been for the fact that God was mercifully walking through these times with each of us, we could have flown apart as a church and left a negative witness for the unbelieving community to point to and jeer. God knows they've wanted to. The world would love for us to fail, and they're thrilled when we don't. It is a paradox.

The purpose in telling this whole story is this: if you ever expect to get anywhere in God's special services, you are going to have to bite the bullet, and force yourself to communicate with every one of the soldiers God has placed around you. As you dive into the ongoing work of God there will no doubt be fellow commandos whom you naturally don't enjoy being around. You don't like the way they look, the way they handle their kids, and maybe you dislike the sound of their voices. Perhaps their life style is opposite to yours, so much so that you cannot even imagine how they can live with themselves. Their tastes turn you off, their hobbies seem absurd to you, and on top of all of these things, the pastor seems to spend more time with them than he does you. All of this can make for a very hard time for you. So what are you going to do?

Maybe this person has developed the habit of noisily coming into home group meeting each week right at the time you are usually presenting your special contribution to the meeting. It seems they are always interrupting you. Are you going to let your feelings fester? No, no—be quick to go to them privately, and in gentleness and meekness share your honest feelings with them. It's that simple, and usually that will be all it requires. You see, most people are not aware when they are offending someone, and if they were made aware of it in a gentle, loving way, they would go to great lengths to correct the problem. But what do we do? We hold grudges against them and never let them know why. How sad.

> Moreover if thy brother shall trespass against thee, go and tell him his fault in private: if he shall hear thee, thou hast gained thy brother. (Matt. 18:15)

If we would all just obey this scriptural instruction, in the spirit of Galatians six, verse one, we would be so much further along as the Church of Jesus Christ.

> Brethren, if a man be overtaken in a fault, ye which are spiritual, restore such a one in the spirit of meekness; considering thyself, lest thou also be tempted.

As you approach your brother or sister with a grievance or some advice, do so remembering that you're not such a spiritual hot rod either, and you may be totally wrong in your evaluation of them. Approach them with an understanding heart, and seek to believe the best. Look for ways to help them and build them up, not to tear them down. And if you are going to go to them, you must be willing to commit yourself to them by offering redeeming help for how ever long it takes. Offer to work with them and don't leave them dangling by themselves. Do not be one who rapidly approaches the intended target, drops a bomb of accusation and condemnation, and then zooms out of sight just as quickly. Do unto others as you would have them do unto you.

Now a word to those of you who are in the position of receiving correction. The Scriptures obligate you to receive your brother or sister in the spirit of humility. You are to esteem them as being better than you are (Phil. 2:3), and seek to make it easy for them to unload their grievances. If you swell up with pride every time a brother or a sister comes to you with something you may be doing wrong, you become a disgrace to God. You are not so good that you can't be corrected by a fellow-heir of Jesus Christ. They may be coming to you with the very bit of advice you need, so receive them in love and seek to understand them. Hear what they are saying, and if you have any questions, ask them.

After your brother or sister has presented the problem to you, thank them for coming to you and release them from any fears they might have that you don't receive them. But make it clear to them, if there is still any question in your mind, that you need time to pray seriously over this matter, and seek the Lord, to find out from Him if you have been in the wrong. Remember, Jesus has the final say, and if we will seriously seek His counsel, He will cause us to see the absolute—not the vague.

You will not go far in this Kingdom's service if you fail in the area of communication. On any battlefield, in any war, open lines of communication between members of the same side are essential. Without open and frank communication, even with the unlovely ones of our group, we are doomed to fail somewhere down the line. True, it may hurt us a little if our brother is totally honest with us about what he's seeing and how he's feeling, but if we will remain open to him, we'll become a much better person for it.

> Open rebuke is better than secret love. Faithful are the wounds of a friend, but deceitful are the kisses of any enemy. (Prov. 27:5–6)

Secret love will seek to conceal, hide, and sweep grievances under the rug. Eventually the grievance makes its way to other folks and the matter grows worse. Somewhere during this time, the person holding the grudge becomes the enemy of the other person. But true love is faithful to send the one with the grievance to his friend to administer private rebuke, which may be wounding for a time, but is eventually healed and truly forgotten. Hearty counsel is as ointment and perfume that rejoices the heart (Prov. 27:9). It may contain rebuke and admonishment at times, but there will be praise and encouragement mixed in too. It's called the sweetness of a friend's counsel.

> He that rebukes a man will afterward find more favor than he who flatters with the tongue.

I have seen men flatter one another with sweet-sounding words, while all the time they despised one another because they never settled their differences when they were small ones. If they would have, today they would probably be the best of friends, highly favoring one another.

Another verse says that if you "rebuke a wise man, he will love you" (Prov. 9:8b). I have found that my most trusted friends—those whom I love the most—are the ones who came to me with their grievances early so that we could work them out. And do not misunderstand that word "rebuke." We often think that word must be administered with a clap of thunder before it can be classified as bonafide rebuke. Not so! While it is true that rebuke often means "sharp disapproval," it more often than not can be administered in very diplomatic ways. Seek to be diplomatic in your dealings with your brothers and sisters.

Communicate! Communicate! Husband, keep your wife abreast of everything that's happening in your life. Wives, do the same with your husbands. Husbands, find the time to sit down regularly and listen to your wife, for she may have much to offer you. I know that my wife, time and time again, has proven to be a wellspring of wisdom to me. I cherish her insight, and the advice she so freely gives to me. So many times it is just what the doctor ordered. I deem men foolish who won't take the time to talk to their wives and listen to them. Their wives may have just the word they are looking for, but they may never get it because they are so wrapped up in the nonessentials of life.

> Oftentimes when I am abnormally burdened with problems, and have no clear answer as to what I am to do, I sit down with my wife, Darlene, and allow her to minister to me.

79

We usually go into the living room and sit together on the couch.

She will scratch my head or massage my neck and shoulders and tell me what a wonderful husband I am and what a mighty man of God I have come to be.

In time we begin to discuss the nature of the problems I am facing and begin to look at possible answers. During these calm, quiet times, Darlene brightly shines with counsel from our all-wise God. I really hate to think where or what I would be without her at my side. She is always there to lift me up when I fall (Eccles. 4:10) and my heart safely trusts in her (Prov. 31:11). Many daughters have done virtuously, but Darlene surpasses them all.

Every once in a while I'll come home sorely vexed with thoughts of discouragement that are so strong I want to quit the ministry. At these times, Darlene has been a priceless source of encouragement to me. She is a very discerning person and easily recognizes when my discouragement is demonically influenced. Rather than being so blunt as to tell me that I am listening to a demon, although at times she has done this, she usually converses with me in such a way that I come to that realization myself. She is very clever in this and by the time she brings me to that conclusion, I am ready to do something about it. During all this time, she is usually scratching my back and pampering me.

You may be thinking this is absurd. To you it might be, but to me it is essential.

Don't get the idea that this is all one-sided because it's not. I endeavor to minister to her in similar ways.

The rigors of being a multi-talented mother and a pastor's wife sometimes take their toll on her. At such times I minister to her, and lift her up. We have adopted the phrase "body ministry" to describe what we do for each other in times of difficulty. We minister to each other physically and spiritually. We touch each other and above all, we communicate.

So be certain to communicate with your spouse. Communicate with your children. Communicate with your parents. Develop an open line of communication with your immediate superior in the church—whether he be a home group leader or the pastor. Be quick to speak the truth in love to everyone with whom you are called to build God's Kingdom. Do not allow the soil of "non-communication" to become the ground in which Satan can sow his destructive seeds of discord.

A way to deal with the problem of poor communication is by employing the use of a calandar. This proved to be a lifesaver in the church in Monterey. In order to stay abreast of what is happening in the lives of my key men, I began to schedule a private breakfast with each of them, once a month. With the breakfast date committed to our calendars we were bound to get together for the much-needed times of fellowship which are so essential to building and maintaining healthy relationships. During this special time, usually in a private booth of a local restaurant, I am able to instill vision, field grievances, or ideas, and generally keep my fingers on the spiritual pulse of the men. They in turn are to share what is happening with their wives.

When I see that two people in our church are having trouble understanding one another, I usually insist that they begin to have breakfast together on a regular basis. I am convinced that if they would just begin to communicate with one another, and get to know each other's hearts, that a lot of their problems would go away.

The benefit of a breakfast is that a good meal can serve to relax the two as they begin to work at building their relationship stronger.

There are any number of ways in which people can begin to work at communicating with each other, but one essential which cannot be ignored is the use of a calandar. With a calandar you will be sure to schedule this valuable time into your busy life.

As the leader of a team of people committed to the building of the Kingdom of God, I am instructed of God to have men and women with me who are determined to maintain open lines of communication with me, and with each other. As a matter of fact, I will not tolerate strife within the ranks. Through years of observation I can honestly say that if people will be quick to communicate with one another in an open and diplomatic way, strife will be nipped in the bud almost every time.

7

Commando Leaders

The successful special service men and women must give much of their credit to their commanding officers. All crack commando troops have someone who marshals their efforts at destroying enemy strongholds and liberating captives. We have been looking at the elite of God, but have yet to examine who His leaders are. Who marshals the special forces for the Lord?

Ephesians gives a list of offices in which you will find most commando leaders operating:

> And He gave some as apostles, and some as prophets, and some as evangelists, and some as pastors and teachers. (Eph. 4:11, NAS)

The five offices listed here are often referred to as the "Five-fold Ministry," and are being restored to the Church in our time. For many centuries such titles as apostle and prophet were ignored, and even relegated to the first-century church. But the Word of God states very clearly that God "has set them in the church" (1 Cor. 12:28), and nowhere does it state that they were removed. As a matter of fact, Ephesians 4:12–13 says they are set in "for the perfecting of the saints for the work of the ministry . . . till we all come in the unity of the faith, and unto the measure of the stature of the fulness of Christ!" This has not been fulfilled as of yet, so therefore we need *all* of the ministry gifts—all of the offices in tack. If they are not in tack the full maturity of the Church will not be realized.

All consistently successful commandos are under the supervision of a leader. In the Body of Christ this leadership position is filled by a pastor (locally), and/or an apostle (translocally). Every elite commando warrior needs a leader to whom he can be accountable. Accountability is a fine "checks and balances" system. We are not talking bondage here (we answer ultimately to Jesus), but we are insisting that every believer be humble enough to allow older, more mature men with proven ministries to speak counsel and wisdom into their lives as the need for these arises.

Had the late A.A. Allen had a man or a group of men to whom he could have been accountable, he may not have died as an alcoholic. Had the late Hobart E. Freeman had men who could have freely spoken counsel into his life, he may not have gotten into error. The facts speak for themselves. You see, the Bible says that in the multitude of counselors there is safety. Perhaps you don't need a multitude all the time, but you do need *someone*.

The great thing about God's law of accountability is that you are allowed to maintain your individuality. You can have a ministry, and launch out and be led by the Spirit of God, but when you begin slipping off into trouble, someone can come to you to correct you without having to be afraid of your rebuking them. This thankless job should definitely be the right of the God-appointed pastors and apostles. No man is to be an island, nor is any ministry. God does not want "Lone Rangers" taking His Gospel to the world. Such men are unconnected to everyone else. I firmly support the teaching that every apostle, every prophet, every teacher, and every evangelist be based in a valid New Testament church somewhere. The day is coming also, when every true New Testament church will be rightly related to an apostle, or apostles, and an apostolic team.

Let us look at the ministry of the apostle, and his apostolic team. The Bible is rich in information concerning this lost office. Thank God, it's no longer lost, but is being restored in this present hour.

THE APOSTLE

The Apostle Paul's ministry tells us much about the role of the apostle. In the book of Acts we find how his apostolic ministry all began:

> Now there were in the Church that was at Antioch certain prophets and teachers; as they ministered to the Lord, and fasted, the Holy Ghost said, Separate me Barnabas and Saul for the work whereunto I have called them. And when they had fasted and prayed, and laid their hands on them, they sent them away. So they, being sent forth by the Holy Ghost, sailed to Cyprus. (Acts 13:1–4a)

History reveals that the church at Antioch was Paul's home church, and was where he labored and put down roots as a Christian. He became a teacher or a prophet—or both. As he was diligent in small, sometimes mundane labors, God counted him faithful (1 Tim. 1:12). Sometime during his stay here, or even perhaps earlier in his Christian walk, he began to hear the call to apostolic ministry. As time went on, the call grew stronger, enabling him to hear it loud and clear. The Bible said that the Holy Ghost "had called them." That speaks of something He had done in the past. However, the call and the time when one is actually sent forth to fulfill that call are often two different happenings. So it was with Paul. He knew that one day he would be launched out into apostolic ministry, but before then he was to prepare, and be faithful in the church at Antioch.

Finally the day came when the church leaders in Antioch were instructed by the Holy Spirit to lay hands upon him and send him forth into the work which he had been prepared for. On that day, Paul's work, and authority, became translocal—for he was sent out, sent away from his local church—in order to fulfill the call of an apostle on his life.

From this passage of the Scriptures we can readily see that apostleship:

1. Originates with God.
2. Is recognized and projected by leaders in a local church, *as* the Holy Spirit wills, and *when* the Holy Spirit wills.
3. Requires that a man be in good standing in a local church; accountable and in tune.
4. Requires that a man already walk in one or more of the other four offices listed in Ephesians 4:11.

Moving on, let us consider the role, or function of the apostle. Paul's first letter to the Corinthians gives a fine start in answering this question.

According to the grace of God which is given unto me, as a wise masterbuilder, I have laid the foundation, and another builds upon it. (1 Cor. 3:10)

Paul gives to us a clear description of what an apostle's unique role is. The word translated "masterbuilder" literally means architect. An architect is one whose profession is to prepare plans for edifices, and exercise a general superintendence over their erection. He designs and frames complex structures, beginning with the proper foundation. He plans and constructs, as to achieve a desired result. Therefore, he has a definite strategy.

The Church of Jesus Christ is compared in several passages of the Scriptures to a building. The clearest of these is found in Ephesians:

Having been built upon the foundation of the apostles and prophets, Christ Jesus Himself being the corner stone, in whom the whole building, being fitted together is growing into a holy temple in the Lord; in whom you also are being built together into a dwelling of God in the Spirit. (Eph. 2:20–22, NAS)

The Church, being built into the very dwelling of God, is to be an eternal dwelling place. This fact necessitates that it not be slipshod, carried out by unqualified personel. God is exceedingly "house proud," and a job as important as this one must not be left to chance. Therefore, God has instituted the job of being architect to the apostle. Apostles walk in measures of anointing that local pastors do not. Thank God for pastoral anointing—but quite frankly, it's not enough.

An apostle can operate as an effective one because God has gifted him that way. It's nothing he can brag about. Paul said, "According to the grace which is given to me" (1 Cor. 3:10). The word "grace" is the greek word *"charis."* It denotes something given as an unearned gift. In this case it refers to apostolic anointing. Paul is saying that all he is, and all he can do, is because of God's unmerited *"charis."* Nevertheless, only one person can efficiently do the work of an apostle, and that is an apostle. If any other office attempts to take the place of the apostolic anointing and ministry, there will be eventual failure. Much of Christendom today is pathetic because of this very thing. When a God-anointed man is replaced by a man-appointed organization and committee, vain religion results.

The biblical apostle is a man with an undeniable call from God (Gal. 1:1; 1 Tim. 1:1), who is sent forth by the leaders of a local congregation under the direction of the Holy Spirit (Acts 13:1–4) for the purpose of overseeing the establishment of new communities of believers. He may also be given the responsibility of giving direction and oversight to churches that haven't been brought into being directly through his ministry (Rom. 1:10–11; Col. 2:1). In cases like this he will always come in because of the invitation of elders in that local church.

Nowadays, there are many churches that are struggling along from one major problem to the next because they began with the wrong foundation. When the foundation of any building is wrong, the building itself will be wrong and will not stand the storms of time. Churches like these must seek God for apostolic authority.

The Word tells us that the Church is to be established upon the foundation of apostles and prophets, Jesus himself being the chief cornerstone. Most churches have Jesus as the cornerstone, but they've neglected the fact that they need to be rightly related to an apostolic team (Eph. 2:20–22). Only the God-gifted apostle can lay the kind of foundation that will last. A local pastor cannot do this! Remember, Paul said that as a wise masterbuilder, he had laid the foundation, and another was building upon it. Apostles lay the foundation for any church, and God-appointed pastors build upon it. If we stray from this pattern, as many thousands have done, we will suffer for it.

Another unique feature of the apostle's ministry is that he is usually in charge of a team of people who work with him. They may travel with him all the time, or they may come in occasionally under his leadership to help him do the job of building the church in any given locality.

The apostle has men and women of special call and anointing within his team. Many of these team members are potential leaders who are getting on-the-job training as they work with the apostle and each other. Prophets often accompany an apostle. Teachers are on the team. Evangelists, and/or people who are motivated evangelistically are usually always with the team. The team is a very anointed one and it takes a special man to head it up. He has to be a discerner of resources and he must recognize God's provision in the people who work for him. He recognizes the anointings on the various people he is associated with—the one gifted as a teacher, or the evangelist, or those who have the ministry of helps. He isn't deceived by those grasping at leadership, and who are seeking to promote their own personal ministries at the expense of the others on the team. The apostle is a good judge of character.

Flattery does not deceive him as it might other men in leadership positions. The unique anointing placed by God upon the apostle should be able to help him see right through wrong motives. In Samaria, Philip was accompanied by a very charismatic man—Simon, the converted sorcerer (Acts 8:5-24). Upon meditating on this passage of Scripture I became aware that Simon accompanied him for many days, and was perhaps a tremendous asset to Philip's ministry. After all, the folks in Samaria already looked up to him, and had done so for some time—as the great power of God! When the apostles Peter and John came on the scene, with their apostolic anointing, they were able to see right through Simon's deceitfulness and "nail him to the wall." Had they not corrected the situation, Simon just might have become the leader of the young, vulnerable church in Samaria. Thank God for His provision of apostles.

The apostle is a complete Church-builder in that he can present the gospel to sinners with authority and anointing. He comes to them with the signs of an apostle which are "signs, wonders, and mighty deeds done with patience and perseverance" (2 Cor. 12:12). He sees that converts are baptized in water and the Holy Ghost (Acts 19:1-6); that they receive an impartation of spiritual gifts (Rom. 1:11); that they are established in a local church complete with a plurality of elders and deacons.

The apostle and his anointed team are complete Church-builders—from foundation to roof. Paul told the church at Corinth that they were the open attestation (seal) that he could do what an apostle had to be able to do (1 Cor. 9:1-2).

His anointed team went about "turning the world upside down" (Acts 17:6), and leaving in their wake, a score of valid New Testament communities of believers.

Once the apostle leaves, the brunt of authority for guiding and directing the ongoing ministry of the church, is placed in the hands of the local pastors. It is not that the apostle no longer has a major part to play in the future of the church (because he does), but it is just that his authority has shifted somewhat. He is no longer present, speaking daily to the saints.

My dad was once the direct and ever-present authority over me—both when I was a child and when I was a teenager. He always had the final say in my life. I can see now that I needed that. But eventually he saw it was time to release me into adulthood. Before long I was married and had begun to raise a family of my own. I fathered two boys, ran my own household, and pursued my own calling in life. My household was under *my* hands-on authority, not my dad's. However, because he had gotten me started in life, and had taught me how to live, and has a tremendous investment in my life, because he is my father and the grandfather of my kids, he has the God-given right, and I make him welcome, to come into my house at any time of any day, in order to offer advice, correction, encouragement, direction, etc. Ultimately the choice to heed his instruction is left to me. I don't have to hear and obey, but I should seriously consider it. I should esteem his counsel as being very important, and actually cherish it. After all, he is the patriarch of my family. His wisdom and experience are two gifts I need at many times in my life particularly if he is a Christian.

This is precisely the role that apostles are to play after they leave the churches they are privileged to plant. The church begins to function on its own and he no longer has his hands on its steering wheel. However, the elders lovingly respect and desire his counsel and overall guidance for the years to come. After all, he is their spiritual father (1 Cor. 4:15).

What if trouble arises? Suppose two out of three of the elders get "out in left field" (spiritually speaking) and begin leading the church way off course? I believe the single elder and the flock have the right and the responsibility to call the apostle and his anointed team for help. If, in the team's eyes, the other two elders are way off in error; and if the one remaining elder and church are looking to the apostle for direction, then the apostle and his gifted team must exercise their God-given authority and administer the necessary discipline, even if it goes as far as excommunication.

What would be permissible should the apostle get way off course and in obvious error? How should the elders of one of his churches respond? Paul instructs us first to entreat him as a father. In a spirit of meekness and redemption the apostle should be corrected (1 Tim. 5:1; Gal. 6:1). If after this, he chooses to pursue his ill-fated course, I believe leaders in other

respected apostolic teams ought to be sought. Perhaps
could bring him to his senses. If not, then the church has
right and responsibility to sever all connections with the wa,
ward apostle and his team.

What we see is that no person is obligated to follow anyone,
even if it is an elder or an apostle—into the pit of hell! But as
far as it depends on you, live in harmony with all men—especially your leaders.

What about the apostle's role and ministry within a church
that wasn't brought into being through his ministry? Many
churches today were started without any apostolic ministry
and anointing involved, and they are really suffering the consequences. Still others that started the same way have seen their
senior pastor's ministry evolve into that of an apostle. His
calling is now taking him into translocal work, starting new
churches. This has been the case with many men.

But what of those churches that are in trouble? They need an
apostle and his team to come into their midst for however long
it takes, and "set things in order" (Titus 1:5). Denominational
boards and committees will never be able to do it because they
lack anointing. An anointed evangelist and a three-week revival won't do it because evangelists cannot get to the foundation and correct things there. It can only be done by the
anointed man called an apostle, and his apostolic team.

As a man of supernatural means, he enters the scene with a
strategy that has its origins in God. Nothing is left to chance
and, as an architect, he follows a blueprint called the Word of
God. He will not tolerate compromise or falsehood (Rom.
16:17; 2 Thess. 3:6,14). As one anointed to work at the
grassroots level, he inspects the foundations of the crippled
church. He knows he must re-lay the foundation in the proper
way in order to insure the ongoing success of the church. Some
of his decisions may seem drastic, but the results will be worth
it in the long run.

Whether the church is one the apostle started from scratch,
or one he adopted in order to rescue it from certain death, he
must retain the right to come in whenever the Lord instructs
him, and inspect the church's foundations and walls. If the

91

the local church are wise and humble men,
's professional input into their local work.
characteristic of the anointed apostle of
xcitement over the advancement of the
His zeal and enthusiasm will actually rub off
people. He equips the church to be apostolic—to
expand its vision, and dream big.

An apostle from Kenya, East Africa, who at the time of this writing has already been used of God in the establishment of over 100 churches, was a guest in my home recently. I am a much better man for it. I can see much more clearly the vision God has for the Church in these days. That man's apostolic vision got all over me—enhancing the picture God had been giving me for quite some time. It is true: if you hang around an apostle long enough, you'll get church-planting on the brain. It is great!

Let us all commit to pray that the valid, New Testament ministry of the apostle be provided and also gladly received in this day of restoration.

The Prophet

In Numbers 11:10–29, we find the story of Moses' appointment of seventy men, elders among their people, who were from that time forward, to stand with Moses in bearing the awesome burden of leading the massive company of God's people. As Moses and the chosen men sat "round about the tabernacle," God took of the Spirit that was upon Moses, and distributed it among the elders. Immediately they began to prophesy without ceasing.

At the same time, two of the seventy remained in the camp, among the people, and prophesied heartily to them. One young man thought it necessary to run to Moses and tell the matter so that it might be stopped. Moses' reply is worthy of note, for he said, "Are you envious for my sake? Would that all of the Lord's people were prophets, and that the Lord would put His Spirit upon them!" Moses thought it a wonderful idea that there be an adequate supply of prophets ministering among the people of God. I believe Moses had God's heart on the matter—for that time, but also for today.

As one of the foundation stones mentioned in Ephesians 2:20, upon which the Church is to be built, the prophet has been terribly neglected, and hindered in carrying out his duties "among the people." And I might stress that a true prophet will go among the people. He may spend much time alone, living in the heights with the Lord, but he will also spend enough time down in the valley, declaring "Thus saith the Lord!" Jeremiah, one of the greatest prophets of all time, stated that he had "a fire burning in his bones, and that he couldn't hold it in or keep it to himself" (Jer. 20:9 TLB). The fire that burned so deeply within him was the unadulterated Word of the Almighty! Prophets are aflame with the "now" Word from God for His people, and it is next to impossible for them to keep it concealed for very long.

The New Testament prophet must be based in a local church, and should be linked to an apostle and his team. Even though he may at times minister out on his own, and even lead a short-term team of people, he should always be covered by, and accountable to an apostolic ministry. In many cases, the prophet's ministry will function only on a local basis, and not to the Body of Christ at large. In such cases he will be submitted to the local leadership of his home church, and may himself be one of the plurality of pastors. The weight of the message that the prophet sometimes brings necessitates his need for accountability. Many "Lone-Ranger" prophets are riding about the Body of Christ today, doing much harm because they have allowed no one close enough to them to judge their lives, ministries, and messages. Because the ministry of the prophet is often so spectacular and dynamic, he must carry the responsibility of setting a good example of humility and accountability for the people among whom he ministers. This job of holding the prophet accountable is placed locally in the hands of the pastors of his home church, and other prophets. In the church, prophets, like pastors, are usually found in the plural. Paul said, "Let the prophets speak two or three, and let the others judge" (1 Cor. 14:29). There is not to be one man who does it all. The prophets are in a group, and where one is ministering, others are to exercise judgment. That is the New Testament pattern.

On a broader level, the prophets are to be accountable to the apostle of the flow of which they are a part. Remember, we are not speaking of dictatorial bondage here, but of New Testament security, of the sort that will insure the prophet's effectiveness for the years to come.

The New Testament prophet's role may be varied, and of course, some minister differently than others. But from the Word of God we can get a grand overall picture of what the prophets among us should be doing.

A prophet is definitely found in a sphere of leadership because:

1. He pours fresh insight about God's ways and purposes into the Church. The Word states that "without a vision, the people perish" (Prov. 29:18). The New American Standard Bible says they are "unrestrained"—going to and fro, in every direction, but going nowhere in particular as a whole. Sadly, this is an accurate picture of much of the charismatic church today. Why? Because of the lack of prophetic men and women pouring fresh, supernatural insight concerning God's will, plans, and purposes into the Church.

In Zechariah 4, a vision is given that shows a golden candlestick which typifies the Church. On either side of it is an olive tree. From each olive tree, pure, undefiled oil flows through two golden pipes into the candlestick. The oil typifies the Holy Spirit and His fresh revelation. The olive trees typify the prophets. The light that burns in the Church is kept bright as the prophets pour fresh insight and revelation into it. For this very reason, people will naturally recognize the prophets as strong leaders who are on the forefront of what God is doing, and seeking to accomplish in the Church.

2. In the Old Testament, the prophets represented the people of God in declaring clear, and sometimes alarming messages to the leaders of nations. They were often looked upon as "bearded eccentrics, calamity howlers, and a needless irritation."[1] While his role today may find him occasionally con-

---

[1] Leonard Ravenhill—*America Is Too Young To Die* Bethany House Publishers, 1978.

fronting the leaders of nations, he will more often be found equipping the Church to be the prophetic voice that will confront the nations. We live in a time when we need more than a few lion-hearted prophets who will declare the Word of the Lord. We need the Church triumphant to rise to its feet.

So primarily, the prophet equips the Church to be prophetic. As he ministers among the people of a given congregation, he will not cause them all to become prophets, but motivationally, they will evolve into a prophetic community of believers. He is a very zealous person—and jealous to see God's Word and His honor upheld with no compromise. This characteristic will rub off on those among whom the prophet ministers.

3. Because of what motivates the prophet, you will usually see him on the front lines of spiritual warfare. As one of the first believers to take the fight to the enemy in his trenches, the rank and file of Christian warriors will grow accustomed to seeing the prophet out in front, leading the troops into the fray. Don't envy his position though. Because he is usually one of the first ones out front, he gets shot at the most. Unless you are divinely built for it, it will do you in. You see, a prophet's ministry is a scourge to those who want to compromise the truth. To speak of a popular prophet is a misnomer, an impossibility. He is often the most misunderstood and misrepresented of all Christians.

Jeremiah lamented that he was ridiculed daily, and that everyone was mocking him. He also stated that because God's hand was upon him in prophetic ministry, he was usually alone (Jer. 15:17). Rebuke was his daily cup, because the people did not want to hear the words he spoke. The false prophets of his day cried "Peace, peace!" when there was no peace, but Jeremiah knew the impending judgments of his God. Therefore he spoke the unattractive truth. At times, his words were on the hearts of his listeners as molten metal on their flesh, and he refused to go with the crowd.

Compromise is an ugly word to the prophet. He cannot be bought or sold, and his lifestyle is often like that of one from another world. He lives in the high and lofty presence of Almighty God, and breathes the rarefied air of inspiration. When he came down to minister among the people, Jeremiah delivered a passion-fired message that either created a revival or a riot. A prophet worth his weight will either be heralded or hounded—usually hounded. Because he marches in cadence to the beat of another Drummer, the prophet is usually out of step with society, and sadly, he is often out of step with those of his own kind—believers in God.

In the New Testament days in which we live, the prophet of God is one who brings the new wine of God's presence to burst open the dried-up wineskins of orthodoxy. Those with mere forms of godliness, but who deny the true power from heaven, insist that we become settlers and do things the way they have always been done. The prophets cry, "No!" and dare to blaze new trails for God. If the prophets are allowed to function in the church we will have revival like we have heretofore only dreamed of. If they are continuously hindered in carrying out their ministries we will experience death and corruption.

Any successful apostolic team must give much of its credit to the prophets who minister within it and from out of it. The prophets are those tried and trusted ones who have waited patiently in the presence of God, heard His voice, gotten a baptism of His power, and an authority to deliver His message to a sick church and an already dead world. He births revival and new beginnings, and so is highly cherished by his apostle and team.

I think of the men I have known in years past who were prophets, and it thrills my heart to reflect on what they accomplished for God. Those who were allowed to function in their own local church always kept the presence of God crisp and sweet in their midst. Those were the congregations that were moving out on the Word of God and accomplishing great things. The traveling prophets always seemed to do the most good for the churches that had a multitude of ministries coming to them. I guess its because a prophet is equipped to minister on foundational levels, and that has been where the biggest need has been. Thank God for other types of ministries, but as I have said, only prophets, along with apostles, are equipped to get down to the foundations of the church.

Of the prophets I have thus far been privileged to know and work with, no two of them have been exactly alike. There is no known curriculum that men use to shape the prophet. I believe that God has His own way of shaping the prophet to suit the hour in which he lives. Only a few things are obvious in them all: they are lonely men, private men, intensely passionate men, powerful men, and misunderstood men. They know that they will suffer much rebuke if they are to be a blessing.

Until the church understands that it is the Lord who makes prophets different, it will continue to misunderstand why the prophet lives the way he does, and will, more than likely than not, persecute him. Anyone who is different becomes the object of ridicule and shame, and prophets are different. They God's lone men. They walk alone, pray alone; God makes them alone. And few prophets have not suffered rebuke from a misunderstanding world and an ill-informed Church.

Now all I have said thus far is not to be taken as license by the prophet to remain or even become an irritable grump. And he must remain accountable to other men. He should seek to get along wonderfully with everyone, as long as he doesn't compromise his integrity or the Word of God in order to do so. The prophet, just like anyone else, is responsible to live the life of peace and love toward all men, as far as it depends on him. He is not to go about seeking to make enemies, but we must all realize that the adding up of enemies may be the end result of the message the faithful prophet heralds.

May the Church of this hour stand *with* our prophets, not *against* them. In this hour of restoration let us pray for them to come forth, and be received. Without them, one of the key foundation stones of the Church will be left out of place, and the Church will fail, allowing the world to plunge into more dark ages. Remember, the prophets shed light, and show us the way in which we should go.

The Evangelist

Evangelists are a special breed of Christian in that they are preoccupied with a desire to win the lost. A person called as an evangelist will exhibit such a love for the lost people of the world that he will literally be driven to reach out with the message that Jesus Christ saves, heals, and delivers. All believers should love the lost, and be involved in reaching out to them, but the evangelist will bend over backwards in an effort to win them to Christ.

Evangelists are so consumed with a burden for the lost, that they never allow themselves to become too tied to stationary things. Fancy houses, lawns, and gardens do not occupy much of their time, nor do clubs, organizations, or even churches. True evangelists know that you do not sit in church buildings and wait for sinners to come to you, but that you must go out into the world and find them. The marketplace, the hospitals, the prisons, the civic gathering places, etc., are where the needy are, so this is where the evangelist goes. He is not too interested in impressing the saints of God in church, but aches in his heart for an audience with the lost.

You would not be very wise if you were to set your watch by the evangelist, because his steps are ordered uniquely by the Lord for purposes of apprehending sinners for the Kingdom of God. Because of this he doesn't always know where God is going to be using him at any given time. Sure, he is able to commit to being at certain places at certain times, but his evangelistic bent causes him to be free-wheeling much of the time. As a spiritual paratrooper, he drops in here, and drops in there, forever encountering God-ordained appointments with the lost of this world.

The evangelist may be the leader of a short-term team of evangelistic people, but then again, he may at many times travel alone. His pace would certainly wear the average Christian to a frazzle, because as I said, his call almost drives him to be reaching out to the lost, and with his calling comes a unique ability.

The maturing of saints very much interests the evangelist, but he usually is uncommitted to giving his time to that process. This is why he must be a part of something larger than his own "private" ministry. We firmly believe that all evangelists should be based in a strong and supportive New Testament church, out of which they can be sent to carry on their work, either locally or universally. Every one of them should be readily accountable to the pastors of the church they are a part of, and of the churches to which they travel. Their ministries should also be indirectly monitored by the apostles to which they are accountable, and they should be related to at least one. Without this unique relationship, an evangelist can get himself into a good deal of trouble and/or burn himself out. Allow me to expound on this by example.

I know a young man and his wife who have recently come off the evangelistic trail. They are an extremely talented couple that both sing and play instruments, and he is a truly anointed speaker. Many folks have come to know Jesus through their ministry.

After several hard years on the road, going from church to church all over this country, they simply wore out. Not only did they wear out, but they became dissatisfied with the lack of sincerity and commitment in the people to which they ministered. It seems that myriads of pastors and congregations were using them for all they were worth, and giving them very little in return. They found that the entertainment factor was what placed them in high demand, and that very few of the churches wanted true revival. At best, the members of these many churches got their ears tickled and their consciences salved, but there was no true revival.

It will always be that way. Evangelists are not equipped to initiate revival in the church; prophets are. Prophets speak the now Word of God to the saints to admonish, rebuke, stir-up, encourage, and establish. Prophets and apostles are equipped to deal with foundations; evangelists are equipped to deal with the sinner. The hell-bound sinner is out there in society, not in the church, and that is where the evangelist will be most effective. The sole ministry of the evangelist, when in the church, is to equip the prophet-revived saints to be evangelistic. He will encourage, train, and equip the saints to go throughout society, actively winning the lost. He equips them to be an evangelistic people.

Another sad fact that the evangelistic couple had to face was that if there were a few sinners who were converted as a result of their ministry, they had to leave them in the cold, dead churches in which they preached. The evangelists could not rest assured knowing that their converts would be well cared for in the churches to which they left them. Much of their fruit simply withered on the vines after they left town because the churches were not adept at giving the converts all they truly needed in order to prosper and mature.

The couple also became enslaved to a schedule that was so rigorous that they were not able to endure it. The result was burn-out. They did not lose their marriage like others I have known, but that would have happened had they kept on.

These are a few of the reasons I believe an evangelist should be related to an apostolic team and a strong local New Testament church. Evangelists, particularly if they are relatively young men and women, must be fathered and cared for just like anyone else. Just because they are called and anointed as evangelists does not mean that they are "super saints" and that they have arrived at spiritual maturity. They need, perhaps as much as anybody, to have their ministry and its effectiveness monitored closely by the architects of the church, the apostles. In this way, there will be a minimum of wasted effort, withering fruit, and burn-out. The evangelists can be cared for, encouraged, corrected if needed, prayerfully and financially equipped, and be a part of a plan that is going somewhere. They can flow among inter-related churches, equipping the saints, reaching the lost for these churches, and be on the forefront of church planting wherever the apostles need them.

Evangelists may be a part of the apostolic team, traveling with it, or they may be utilized by the team as they are sent out from it. Either way, they are to be a valuable asset to the overall ministry of the team, and the churches with which they are involved.

Evangelists, whether they be men or women, must be Christians of honest report, filled with the Holy Spirit and God's wisdom, so that they can handle the various situations that will confront them. It would be wrong for pastors and apostles to utilize them if these essentials are not apparent in their lives.

100

The evangelist must also walk in the power of God. No true evangelist is devoid of signs, wonders, and miracles among the people to whom he ministers. If they do not accompany him, at least a great deal of the time, he does not yet have proof that he is an evangelist. It is much better for one to prove he is something, and then be recognized, than for him to claim to be something, and then fail in backing up his claim. Philip did great signs and wonders among the people (Acts 8), but he wasn't called an evangelist until later (Acts 21:8).

Evangelists will flow in the gifts of the Holy Spirit with at least six of the nine gifts operating at various times. His message will be simple (so the ignorant can understand), and yet, the demonstration of God's power will be strong (1 Cor. 2:4). A thorough evangelist will not only seek to win the lost to Jesus, but he will also see to it that they are immersed in water as an outward sign of the work of God's grace in their hearts. He will then see to it that the converts are securely planted in a valid New Testament church where they can hear the whole counsel of God and grow strong in the Lord. If there are no churches of this caliber in the area, then the evangelist should make it known to his apostle (if he isn't already aware of it), and steps will have to be taken toward the formation of a church for the new Christians. Evangelists should not attempt to do this by themselves, as they are not equipped to do it accurately. This is why it is advisable that he be related to a larger work, with an apostle at its head.

Our prayer should be that the evangelists come forth. A world harvest awaits us, and much of it will spoil in the fields if the mighty evangelists of God do not thrust in their sickles. They will equip us, and demonstrate to us exactly how we can be most effective in winning the lost for God. They are destined to come forth in greater numbers than ever before and bring in a great harvest for the Kingdom. As they go forth into the harvest field with mighty signs and wonders done in the name of Jesus Christ, the multiplicity of pastoral people in the church are going to really have their hands full as they care for all the new spiritual babies. It will be wonderful.

The Pastor

Another commando leader operating in the Body of Christ is the pastor. The pastor is an elder, and in the local church there are usually several of them, ranging in number from two to however many are needed, called, and qualified. They are given the local job of feeding and tending the sheep. Other New Testament names given this man are: bishop, shepherd, and overseer. Among these men there is a co-equality of nature, but not a co-equality of authority. There is a pastor among pastors who gives primary direction and leadership. Somebody has to be clearly at the helm. This *does not* mean unilateral leadership (involving one only of several parties). His decisions have to be confirmed, or should be. Unilateral leadership is wrong; there must be plurality.

Headship

Among the pastors there must of necessity be a senior pastor who serves as the head of the local church. God puts "headship" into everything He does. God is the head of the Godhead; Jesus is the head of the Church; the husband is the head of the wife; and the senior pastor is the head of the local church.

The senior pastor is not independent though, and plurality remains. No person is infallible, so everything of importance ought to be done in counsel with others because even the person with the gift can be wrong sometimes. The council at Jerusalem is a fine example of headship within a plurality. The Lord used James to say, "My sentence is," and the others said, "It is the Lord" (Acts 15:1–22). There must be steerage on any vehicle that is going anywhere.

There must be a co-equality of nature, however. All pastors are to have a "shepherd's heart." They are to strengthen and mature the relationships of the individual believers with Jesus, teaching them to hear His voice (John 10:27) through the various ways He speaks to them. They are to build strong, harmonious relationships between the members of the flock (1 Thess. 5:12–13).

At no time should a human pastor attempt to interpose himself between the sheep and the Lord Jesus. They must remember that Jesus is to have complete and total Lordship over the lives of every soul for which He gave His life. And at no time is a pastor to interpose himself between the sheep and the other pastors. This has happened in the past and the damage that resulted was irreparable.

The qualifications which must be met before a man can even be considered for the pastorate are quite tough. He must first be placed in that position by the Lord himself. If he is not clearly placed in that position, but undertakes to fill it anyway, without the proper anointing, he will fail. Even if he does seem to be good at it (by his own ability) he will one day be judged in light of what he should have done with his life. That's why Peter exhorts us to "make our calling and election sure" (2 Pet. 1:10). I have seen young men and women detect a call on their lives, and automatically assume they should become pastors. So they run off to a seminary and train for the pastorate, and then hope to get appointed to a church by their denomination. In time they are placed, and they begin to experience a life of hell on earth, because God didn't equip them to be a pastor. What they should have been taught was to look into the other ministries in the Body of Christ, and determine exactly what the Lord wanted them to do. This takes a little time and, besides, God wants us to make our calling and election *sure*.

The other qualifications of the New Testament pastor are listed in 1 Tim. 3:1–7 and Titus 1:6–9.

> Some fairly stiff requirements are found in these two passages, and unless you understand why they are listed, you may become disheartened and/or embittered by them.
>
> Recently I was given the responsibility of discipling a man who was equipped with a great personality and natural leadership qualities. By nature he was an extrovert who loved being with people and thoroughly enjoyed helping them. He had a keen mind and was very sensitive to spiritual stimuli. A desire to be a leader was present in him and I detected it on the very first day I met him.
>
> He quickly developed a firm grasp of the Word of God and so became an accurate dispenser of knowledge and

wisdom for those around him. People automatically began to look to him as one of those who could give them answers in their times of questioning.

Perhaps you are wondering if I put him into a significant leadership position since he was endued with so many excellent qualities. The answer to that is no. I failed to inform you that all of these praiseworthy qualities were found in him even before he was a year old in the Lord. The Bible clearly warns not to put a novice into a substantial position of leadership because of the tendency to pride (1 Tim. 3:6).

Another factor that I came to bear heavily on his situation was that his wife was not a believer and was, in fact, antagonistic toward his new-found faith. He had a desire to lead his children into the things of God, but his wife even resisted him in that. The result was that he didn't have his children in subjection to him nor did he have a home in which he could be totally hospitable to guests—two prerequisites to proper leadership within the Church of Jesus Christ. Well-disciplined kids are essential to good hospitality because they help to determine the atmosphere of the home. Is it peaceful or is it an anarchy?

The day came when he read those qualifications listed in Paul's writings. He saw all that was hindering him and became disheartened and eventually embittered. He grew to resent the fact that the qualifications were in Paul's writings and also began to question whether Paul's writings were literally the word's of God.

Thank God, I caught it in time. I helped him to see that the qualifications are listed there not to hold anyone back, but that they may come forth properly, in the right manner and at the right time. My younger Christian brother was viewing those essential qualifications for eldership as hindrances designed to hold him down and hold him back forever. He saw his situation as being hopeless. What I had to do was change his focus and help him to see it from a different perspective.

I encouraged him to aim for God's best. His desire for leadership was good and healthy, and I wanted to see him come forth into it. But a few things had to happen first, and a few things had to be taken care of. We would work and pray together to see these things change, and by faith we knew they would change.

Once he saw that I wanted him to come forth, and not attempt to hold him down by the use of Paul's list of qualifications, his mind was set at ease. Now we simply do all we know to do and wait patiently for God to do what only He can do in the life of my brother's wife. We will use Paul's qualifications as a safe guideline and will at all times seek to apply sanctified common sense to the situation. Already God has done wonders, and I can thankfully say that my brother is at peace with himself and with God. The day is coming when he will shine brightly as a leader in God's Kingdom because he will not have been exalted to a position of leadership before his time. We need more pastors, and the qualifications listed in Paul's letters to Timothy and Titus are not there to hold people back, but that they might come forth in a manner pleasing to the Lord.

One more interesting note: The Scriptures say that if a man "desires the *office* of a bishop, he desires a good *work*" (1 Tim. 3:1). Many men desire the office and the recognition it brings, but if they knew the *work* involved, they would count the cost a little more thoroughly before grasping the office.

The office of pastor is an honorable position in the Body of Christ, and I long for the day when this important office is filled by no one but God-called, God-anointed, no-compromising men of God who pattern themselves totally after the Chief Shepherd, Jesus Christ.

8

The Need for Character

I have touched on the subject of character only briefly thus far. Now I want to focus on its importance, and how it relates to your ongoing service in God's kingdom.

Many a man of God has barged into elite kingdom warfare well ahead of his time. I have seen such individuals flourish for a season, shine as brightly as the North Star, and then fizzle out almost as quickly as they rose to glory. What went wrong? They lacked true, godly character in their lives.

In today's fast-paced Christianity, there is an abundance of teaching on the good and mighty gifts of the Holy Spirit, as listed in 1 Corinthians 12. I value this teaching. There are few Bible subjects that generate as much excitement as the gifts of the Spirit, and yet there are few Bible subjects that can get a young Christian in as much trouble as the gifts of the Spirit.

Many young, "recognition-seeking" ministers have seen a "charisma" or two as being their ticket to "gospel stardom."

Sadly, the majority of the Christian world flocks to these "greenhorns" in order to see *El Shaddai* do His thing. Often the gullible fans are only treated to seeing the little gospel superstar do *his* thing. If by some stroke of God's mercy, something genuine does happen, it only serves to swell our little star's head all the more. Eventually, he will fall hard, and we probably won't hear of him again.

What was wrong? Though he had a little measure of gifting, he lacked the necessary character. Where was his humility? Did he not learn that God personally resists the proud, and did he really feel he was God's extra-special gift to the masses? This "precious one" should have been patient and more in tune with God's Word on the fruit of the Holy Spirit which has to do with character.

The problem faced here is that gifting can come at the snap of God's finger, if God so chooses to place it (and He often does), but character is fruit that must be cultivated. Fruit needs time to grow. You cannot rush the growth of fruit in your life, any more than you can speed up the growth of fruit in your orchard. It takes time, and God has plenty of patience. We must learn to be patient also.

If there is an insufficient amount of character in your life, there will be an insufficient amount of substance to back up the success of your gifting. Know this: Gifting will bring you success, but it will require character to handle it properly. If I am sounding redundant—good! Repetition only serves to drive this important point home.

God seeks for faithful people to use as His instruments in reaching this lost and dying world. He teaches us that if "we are faithful in little things, He will make us ruler over much" (Luke 19:17, paraphrased).

God wants you to be faithful in doing those mundane, non-glamorous tasks He has given you to do. You need to be a good father and husband. You need to raise your children to be Christians of whom God can be proud. Also, see to it that your wife is fulfilled in her relationship with you, and with God. Learn to be content on the job that you now have, and do your work as unto the Lord. Labor to get your appetite under control. You need to be daily crucifying that bad temper. Get that unruly tongue in line. The list goes on and on.

Granted, God does not wait for perfection before He launches you into ministry, because if He did, none of us would ever go. However, He does search through the leaves of our lives seeking fruit. At least some fruit should be there— growing, maturing, thrilling His Father heart. If it is not there, don't expect God to use you very much. Be patient in what may seem a meager beginning, and let God promote you in His time. (See Zech. 4:10; 1 Pet. 5:6; Ps. 37:5.)

I knew a young man who after one year, dropped out of a two-year Bible school and knew for sure he was to start a church that was to be the biggest church in the Shenandoah Valley of Virginia. He came into the area like gang-busters, quickly gathered a bunch of followers, and presented him-self—God's gift to the Shenandoah Valley.

He never bothered to find out what God had already been doing in the area. He never bothered to seek other men of God, with proven New Testament ministries in the area, to ask for their prayers and support. His badge of authenticity was that a well-known evangelist had once prophesied over him in a mass meeting in the Midwest. This he brayed over the airwaves of the local Christian radio station almost daily. He was clearly a lone ranger, not sent from any local body, out doing his own thing, for his own exalted ego. Needless to say, after a year or two he fell hard, and became the object of much ridicule and shame in that part of Virginia. He then moved on in shame. I believe he's down in Texas now; no doubt he's still trying to build "his" ministry.

Can you see the need for character first, and then a success-ful ministry? Allow God to use your office, home, school, and church to develop the fruit of the Spirit in your life. After a goodly amount of faithfulness, endurance, integrity, and other godly attributes are developed in your life, you can then watch God launch you into more and more ministry. As the great success comes, you'll be more than sufficient to handle it.

One day Jesus sent seventy of His disciples out to preach the gospel of the kingdom, to heal the sick, and so forth. When they returned, after many days, they were as excited as school children and a bit lifted up in pride, because "even the devils were subject to them in Jesus' name!" (Luke 10:17) They now knew from a little bit of experience that Psalms 44:5 was real and true:

> Through thee will we push down our enemies: through thy name will we tread them under that rise up against us. (Ps. 44:5)

As great and wonderful as this was, Jesus detected pride, and checked it in His statement that followed: "I beheld Satan as lightning fall from heaven."

How had Satan been booted out of God's heaven, and for what reason? Pride! The desire to be a big somebody. Jesus knew the consequences of the pride-filled heart. He knew the success that His seventy were experiencing could lead to undue pride if it were to go unchecked. As the late Bishop J.C. Ryle said, "Few Christians can carry a full cup with a steady hand."

Character: an abundance of it is needed in the life of the commando for God. Never forget that as long as you live.

I would not want to finish this chapter on character without stressing to you the utter importance of "completing a job."

As a commando leader myself, I look for this important element of character in anyone who would desire to be a part of my ministry team. If a person is in the bad habit of beginning a job, but not seeing it through to completion, he proves his unfaithfulness. A man or woman of God ought to work diligently to see his or her job through to completion. There can be no excuse for anything else. If an individual is unable to complete the job by himself, he ought to appoint qualified assistance, and see to it that nothing is left undone.

Many who read this book are guilty of this major character flaw. They have begun various jobs with much zeal and vigor, only to grow "weary in well doing" and at last they give up, or go on to something else. The result? A job begun but not finished, and how sloppy and unfaithful this is in the eyes of God. Complete the assignment given you, and be diligent about it.

The eyes of the Almighty are upon you, and He is waiting to see if you will be faithful until the end of the job; if you are, He can trust you with more and better responsibilities.

Fruit and gifting. One deals with the abilities of God in our lives and the other deals with the character of God in our lives. We need both. Just see to it that you do not lag behind in character.

9

The Anointing

When one speaks of the anointing, a large segment of professing Christendom is left in the dark, because they do not understand this word. If one substitutes the word "unction," even more folks are left without understanding. A Christian who lives in ignorance, where anointing is concerned, is at quite a disadvantage. Satan thrives on our ignorance, particularly when it involves the anointing of God for our lives.

Let us look to the Word for greater understanding of the anointing.

But you have an *unction* from the Holy One, and you know all things. (1 John 2:20, italics mine)

But the *anointing* which ye have received of Him abideth in you. (1 John 2:27, italics mine)

The Greek word *chrisma* is translated both as "unction" and "anointing" in the King James Version. W.E. Vine defines it as "an enabling" for believers to possess the knowledge of the truth.[1] As I have studied the Scriptures I have come to realize that the "enabling" of which Vine speaks is much more than simply being able to know the truth, but it is an enabling to effectively walk out and work the truth for the good of those who are bound in any way by Satan's kingdom.

Oil usually symbolizes the anointing. In the Old Testament, whenever a king, a prophet, or a priest was set into his unique office, oil was poured on his head, symbolizing the sanctifying, enabling presence of the Holy Spirit upon his life. The Scriptures speak of "precious ointment [anointing oil] upon the head, that ran down upon the beard, even Aaron's beard; that went down to the skirts of his garments" (Ps. 133:2). From that moment forward, Aaron was particularly "enabled" for his special office, and its functions among God's people. The oil which Moses poured upon his head was an outward sign that the Holy Spirit and His enabling presence were now on Aaron to stand in the office of a priest.

The anointing of God is not merely an "it," but it is "He." The Holy Spirit is the anointing of God. Along with His presence there comes His divine enabling in and through the life of the believer. We are very fortunate in that; as New Covenant people He abides *inside* of us. This is quite a change from what Old Covenant priests, prophets, and kings experienced. In those days the prized anointing came *upon* them to anoint them for certain tasks only, at certain times. However, today He comes to dwell *inside* of us, and He never desires to leave. Jesus once made the statement that the Holy Spirit dwelt *with* His followers, but would one day dwell *in* them (John 14:17b). Thank God, that day has come. Since He made that statement, the price for mankind's redemption has been paid in full, Jesus has ascended to the right hand of the Father, and He has sent the promised Holy Spirit to live inside of all true believers. It is almost too wonderful for the mind to comprehend, and yet, it is true.

---

[1] *W.E. Vine's Expository Dictionary of New Testament Words,* Page 61, Mac-DONALDS PUBLISHING CO.

Now let us examine the ministry of the Holy Spirit through the life of Jesus and the Apostle Paul. The Scriptures record:

How God *anointed* Jesus of Nazareth with the Holy Ghost and with power: who went about doing good, and healing all that were oppressed of the devil; for God was with him. (Acts 10:38, italics mine)

Had Jesus not had the Holy Spirit with Him, He would not have had the anointing and its ensuing power operative in His ministry. Quite frankly, the Father would not have been with Him in power. Those oppressed by the devil would not have been liberated, and all of the good that Jesus desired to do could not have been accomplished. Everything Jesus did in His time on earth was accomplished through the power and anointing of the Holy Spirit. Every message He preached, every scriptural text He taught from, every blind eye He opened, and every demon He cast out, was done by the anointing that abode within Him, and upon Him. God's power was present to heal "all manner of sickness among the people" (Matt. 4:23).

And now let us see what the Scriptures said of Paul:

And God wrought special miracles by the hands of Paul. (Acts 19:11)

God, the Holy Spirit, worked by the anointing through Paul's hands. You could rightly say that Paul had anointed hands; the sick were healed, and demons were forced to leave, because God worked mightily through Paul by the anointing.

Some people argue that miracles passed away when Paul died. They stress that Paul was the last Christian to work miracles, and that when he died, miracles ceased. But, thank God, the Word says that it was *God* who worked the miracles, and He's not dead! It is true that Paul passed away, but God hasn't! He is the same miracle-working God today that He was back then.

Another way to describe the anointing is to speak of being in the power of the Holy Spirit.

And Jesus returned in the power of the Spirit into Galilee. (Luke 4:14)

Early in Luke 4, Jesus is said to have gone into the wilderness "full of the Holy Ghost" (Luke 4:1). He went into the wilderness "full" of the Spirit, and came out of the wilderness "in the power" of the Spirit. I have learned over the years that these are two different states of being. In the case of Jesus it was not until He had spent forty days fasting, praying, reading the Scriptures, and successfully combatting the defeating Satan in the wilderness, that He began to minister in the "power" of the Spirit of God! Not only did Jesus fast, pray, and diligently seek God at the outset of His earthly ministry, but He continued these vital practices until the end of His ministry. Luke 5:16 literally reads that "He was withdrawing Himself into the deserts and praying." This shows that it was a regular practice for Him to get alone with the Father. Had He stopped doing this, He too could have lost power. Jesus Christ of Nazareth was so powerful and successful among the people, because He was so faithful to seek God on the mountaintop, in deserts, and in the solitary places (Matt. 17:1; Mark 1:35; Luke 6:12). No man can be a giant in ministry, and a weakling in prayer. The back side of the desert, or the remote regions of the solitary places are where the bush burns with the message from God that will set people free. It is where the voice is heard, where the vision is given, and where the intimate union to His will occurs. It is as God's men wait upon Him here, that they are immersed in His power, and given heavenly authority to proclaim His message to a needy Church and a world that is galloping to the pit.

Would-be commando for Jesus, until you diligently seek God for His mighty anointing in the same ways your Master did, you simply will not receive it.

As our mentor Ravenhill wrote, "Unction is not a gentle dove beating her wings against the bars outside the believer's heart [trying to get in], rather, she must be pursued, and won! Unction cannot be learned, only earned by prayer! Unction is God's knighthood for the soldier who has wrestled in prayer, and won the victory. It comes not by the laying on of the bishop's hands; neither does it mildew when the [Christian]

116

soldier is cast into prison."[2] Praise God! Unction is being in the power of the Spirit of God.

Evidence of the Anointing

In Ravenhill's classic book, *Why Revival Tarries,* he begins a chapter on unction by telling his readers what it is not. It is not the compromised preaching in much of what is called the church around the world. It is not always the abundance of "Christian" endeavor that you witness in the land. Much of what passes for effective Christian accomplishment is really a poor excuse for what the anointing would produce if it were truly present.

How do I know what it is not? Because I know what it is. The Word of God is clear on the subject.

Evidence of the anointing at work is victory! The evidence of its shows up when the meek and the poor have the gospel preached to them, and God's Word changes their circumstances, and their lives. It is there when the brokenhearted are once again whole, and when the captives have liberty proclaimed to them. It is there when the very prison doors holding the captives are kicked in and the prisoners come forth into freedom. At these times you witness true spiritual anointing at work. As the acceptable year of the Lord is proclaimed, and people begin to walk free of the bondages that have held them, you can rightly say that you have witnessed a good measure of the anointing at work (Isa. 61:1–3; Luke 4:18–19). The anointing is power, and it rattles the foundations of Satan's prison houses to their footings.

Another thing about the anointing is that it not only deals with manifestations of a problem, but it goes to the root of the problem and corrects things there. Mere religion ("strong drink"—Isa. 56:12) deals only with the outward manifestations of much deeper problems. A cyst is an example we can use. One can cover a cyst with gobs of cosmetic cream in a

[2] Leonard Ravenhill; *WHY REVIVAL TARRIES*; 1959; Bethany House Publishers.

117

vain attempt to make it go away, but until the person digs into the center of the thing, and removes its morbid core, he is destined for disappointment.

A few years ago I knew of an alcoholic who was prone to fits of extreme violence while drinking. His wife often had to call the police to lock him up in order to protect both herself and her family. A form of religion was introduced to him by a few religious men in his community, but this only served to cover up the deepest needs of the man's life. At best he was made into a man, tagged with a denominational title, and not into a bona fide disciple of Jesus Christ. Foundational issues such as repentance, the new birth, and water baptism were never taken care of in the man's life. He never received deliverance from alcoholism, nor his violent temper, and within ten years he died from alcohol-related physical problems. "Strong drink" (Isa. 56:12) duped the strong drinker.

Religion feeds a starving man with physical food [and this is good], but it leaves the man empty and desolate in his spirit. This is disgusting in light of the fact that Jesus Christ died on Calvary in order to set our spirits free from spiritual death, not merely outward, physical situations. The anointing always points man to the absolute Lordship of Jesus in his life. Until the yoke of "spiritual bondage" is broken from a slave's neck, you haven't really helped him. A mere form of godliness knows nothing of breaking spiritual yokes simply because it is itself a spiritual yoke of bondage (Gal. 5:1).

God's true anointing will break yokes off the slaves' necks.

> And it shall come to pass in that day, that his burden shall be taken away from off thy shoulder, and his yoke from off thy neck, and the yoke shall be destroyed because of the anointing. (Isa. 10:27)

In this verse from Isaiah, the word anointing can equally be translated as "fatness." As the Word of God is brought into the lives of bound-up men and women, and is received as truth and liberty, it begins to produce faith and substance in their lives. Spiritual "bulk" is increased in the life of the person to the degree that yokes of bondage begin to burst off of them, and fall away. This is something that takes place within the person with the problem. Things inside can be made so nice for God and His Word that the devil will be compelled to leave. But also, a minister of faith and power, can take hold, as it were, in the spirit realm, and break away the yokes from without the prisoner's body. Either way, deliverance can come through the anointing.

The anointing breaks yokes! If there are no yokes being broken, it's because the anointing is not present. Always remember that.

The anointing, when present and free to operate, will always leave a trail of born-again spirits, healed bodies, and renewed, refreshed minds behind it.

In a prison I once laid my hands upon a man to get him saved and baptized with the Holy Spirit. The anointing that night was so strong that it also delivered him from a drug addiction, and brought physical healing to his diseased heart.

I heard about all of these other miracles a week later upon my return to that prison for ministry. I am telling you, there is no limit to what the anointing will do when He is present.

If a person is in need of healing, be it physical or emotional, but is weak in faith, he had better go to where the anointing is flowing. The sick were laid in the streets where they knew Peter would be passing, hoping that only his shadow would fall upon them and they could be healed. Multitudes thronged around Jesus because He was filled with Holy-Spirit anointing, and healings were commonplace. But that is not the end of it. Jesus said:

> He that believeth on me, the works that I do, shall he do also; and greater works than these shall he do, because I go to my Father. (John 14:12)

Jesus is now seated at His Father's right hand, and we should be doing the greater works, but alas, we are not even doing the works He did! The Church of Jesus Christ should be getting more people healed, more of the demon oppressed set free, and more of the lost into the Kingdom of God. What has been wrong? Among other things, we've lacked the anointing.

Another glorious result of the anointing is the evidence of "sanctification" in the anointed one's life. Sanctification means separation unto God, and the holy life that is its result. W.E. Vine writes: "That believers have 'an anointing from the Holy One' indicates that this anointing renders them holy, separating them to God."[3] Only anointing enables one to be so sanctified. Sanctification and anointing. The two feed each other; they go together.

When a person comes to receive Jesus Christ as his personal Lord and Savior, the Holy Spirit does a sanctifying work in his heart. Now he lives to please the Lord. He very much desires to be holy, and if he does not, one should seriously question whether the Holy Spirit did a genuine thing in him. True Christians are divinely set apart unto a life of holiness, and holiness becomes a habit.

Bishop J.C. Ryle wrote, "Holiness is the habit of being of one mind with God, according as we find His mind described in Scripture. We agree with His judgement, hating what He hates, loving what He loves, measuring everything in this world by the standard of the Word of God. He who most entirely agrees with God, he is the most holy man."[4] Bishop Ryle also wrote, "A holy man will endeavor to shun every known sin, and to keep every known commandment. He has a greater fear of displeasing God than of displeasing the world. He knows his heart is like a tinder, and will diligently keep clear of the sparks of temptation. A holy man will strive to be like our Lord Jesus."[5]

When one comes humbly to Jesus, the grace of God gives him enough of a measure of anointing to sanctify him. This sanctification produces the desire to be Christ-like. But the anointing to desire that must be present. Anointing precedes sanctification. See Aaron's example:

[3] *W.E. Vine's Expository Dictionary of New Testament Words*, Page 61, Mac-DONALDS PUBLISHING CO.
[4] J.C. Ryle; *The BEST OF J.C. RYLE*; 1981 Baker Book House—Summit Books.
[5] J.C. Ryle; *THE BEST OF J.C. RYLE*; 1981 Baker Book House—Summit Books.

And he Moses poured the anointing oil upon Aaron's head, and anointed him, to sanctify him, [or, set him apart . . .] (Lev. 8:12)

Notice that Aaron was anointed first, and sanctified second. Only as an anointed and sanctified man could he dare enter into the presence of God to offer sacrifices as a priest. The same holds true for us today. We go to God anointed and sanctified by the precious blood of Jesus, and as New Covenant priests, we offer up to God spiritual sacrifices (1 Pet. 2:5)

How to Increase the Anointing

1. *Give first place to the Word of God in your life.* This takes determination. The more you give yourself to it, the more sanctification is worked out in your life. The more you lead the sanctified life, the more powerful anointing you will walk in. The anointing of God is on the Word of God, it works in unison with the Word of God.

At this time I would like to compare several verses of Scripture so that we can see just how closely linked the anointing of God and the Word of God are.

I have written unto you fathers, because ye have known Him that is from the beginning. I have written unto you, young men, because ye are strong, and the Word of God *abideth in you,* and ye have overcome the wicked one. (1 John 2:14, italics mine)

But the anointing which ye have received of him *abideth in you,* and ye need not that any man teach you: but as the same anointing teacheth you all things, and *is truth,* and is no lie, and even as it hath taught you, ye shall abide in him. (1 John 2:27, italics mine)

Sanctify them through thy truth: thy *Word is truth.* (John 17:17, italics mine)

This is he that came by water and blood, even Jesus Christ; not by water only, but by water and blood. And it is the Spirit that beareth witness, because *the Spirit is truth.* (1 John 5:6, italics mine)

121

From these Scriptures you can readily see that the Word of God, the Spirit of God, and the anointing of God all agree. They are in total unison, and you cannot divorce them from one another. It is when one brings the Word of God together with the Spirit of God in ministry, that the prized anointing goes into effect. When there is no anointing, something has been left out. The Spirit of God is to be in us, to anoint the Word in us. Being maintained full of the Holy Spirit, and building a rich deposit of God's Word in our spirits is essential to increasing the anointing in our lives. There is no other way, and anything else is a poor substitute. All over our land there are believers who exhibit about as much anointing as a gnat, because they underemphasize either the Word of God, or the Spirit of God, or both. Usually both! Without the Word dwelling in you richly, you will not be growing in freedom yourself, and you will be diminished in those things which are so necessary to effective Christianity. You will be slipping spiritually, and consequently will lose power.

2. *Increase the anointing by fasting.* Jesus himself told us that there are certain kinds of demons that will not be compelled to leave a person unless the deliverance minister lives the fasted life (Mark 9:29). This does not mean you should starve yourself, but you should devote a certain amount of time to fasting. I like to do it periodically. The great man of faith, Kenneth E. Hagin, fasted one day a week, every week, for years and years. He said he grew in the stature of the Lord more in those years than at any other time in his life. Look at the results. Hagin's influence is felt the world over.

It is told that the great John Wesley would not ordain a man into the ministry unless he vowed to fast breakfast and lunch, every Wednesday, and Friday.

It is extremely important for God's elite commandos to adopt a regular schedule of fasting. Each should pray, perhaps experiment a little, and definitely find which schedule best suits them.

The Scriptures say that the fast that pleases God is designed to "loose the bands of wickedness, to undo the heavy burdens, and to let the oppressed go free, and that ye break *every* yoke"

(Isa. 58:6). Remember, the yoke is broken because of the anointing (Isa. 10:27), and it requires a certain amount of fasting in one's life to secure a strong anointing.

3. *A corollary with fasting is the word humility.* David humbled his soul with fasting (Ps. 35:13), and thus he became known as "a man after God's own heart."

Humility is so important in the life of the Christian soldier. The Word of God abounds with teaching that shows that the proud get nowhere with the Lord. God actually sets himself *against* the prideful, and sees to it that they are brought to nothing. My brother or sister, if you want to go far in God, humble yourself with fasting.

4. *To experience the anointing of God consistently throughout your lifetime, see to it that it flows from a holy and pure life.* It is written that Jesus, "loved righteousness, and hated iniquity," and that because of this, God anointed Him with the oil of gladness [joy and strength] above His fellows (Heb. 1:9). The oil of gladness speaks literally of "joy," and Nehemiah 8:10 says, "The joy of the Lord is your strength," or "strong anointing." If you are filled with both the Word and Spirit of God, you will literally hate sin in your life. You will not tolerate it, but you will love leading a righteous life before God. The glorious result of these proper attitudes, produced as they are by the Word and the Spirit of God, will always be a strong anointing, just like it was in Jesus' life! The strength of your joy, and its accompanying anointing, is determined by the strength of your righteous life. Stay close to God: in His Word, in prayer, in holiness, because "in His presence is fulness of joy" (Ps. 16:11).

Ecclesiastes exhorts us to "Eat the bread [Word] with joy, and drink of the wine [the Holy Spirit] with a merry heart; for God now accepts our works [our labor is not in vain in the Lord]. Let thy garments be always white; and let thy head lack no ointment [anointing]" (Eccles. 9:7–8). Notice how the Word, the Spirit, clean garments, and an unlimited anointing go hand in hand? It is all over the Word, my beloved. Hate the garment spotted by the flesh, especially if you are the one wearing it! If you do not develop a hatred for sin in your flesh, you will be rendered powerless down the home stretch. Yea, you may not even make it home. Jesus said that in the church in Sardis, there were only a few, a small handful, who had not "defiled their garments." He said that these few "shall walk with me in white: for they are worthy" (Rev. 3:4). Wow! That certainly is sobering.

5. *To walk in the anointing of God in a consistent manner it will be absolutely necessary for you to put on the priestly garments of the child of God.* In Exodus 28 and 29 we find Aaron and his sons putting upon themselves consecrated garments so they could be anointed.

As Christians we have been "robed in a robe of righteousness" (Isa. 61:10), in that Jesus is now our righteousness. We have also been exhorted to "put on the garment of praise" (Isa. 61:3). We have been issued the whole armor of God" (Eph. 6:13), and we are to "put on zeal as a cloak" (Isa. 59:17), because that is what Jesus did, and we are to follow His example. As you live in these priestly garments, anointing will saturate your life through and through.

As Christians we are a royal priesthood, chosen of God, to do exploits for His cause in the earth. Aaron and his descendants didn't "have anything on us"; as a matter of fact, we've got one up on them, because we are the priests of a "better covenant that is established upon better promises" than the one they had (Heb. 8:6). But as it was with them, so it is with us: if we do not put on the priestly, anointed garments that the Lord makes available for us to wear, we will not be able to function adequately in our covenant office. Put on the garments of God.

6. *Simple obedience is another essential for increasing the anointing in one's life.* God has said that "to obey is better than sacrifice" (1 Sam. 15:22). The Christian warrior cannot go through life consistently disobeying the instructions of the Lord, and expect to minister in an anointing. At this moment the Lord is speaking to each one of us, telling us what He would have us do or not do. We had better obey Him; it's so much better for us to do so. Then the anointing will work mightily.

7. *Along with obedience, there is the importance of follow-ing Jesus' command to "go!"* If we do not obey this command we will not see the anointing breaking bondages over people's lives, for it is as we "go," that God "confirms His Word with signs following" (Mark 16:15–20). Notice that the signs *follow* us, not *go ahead* of us. If we don't go, nothing will be accom-plished.

I once heard Evangelist Jerry Savelle say, "Your *go* may not be any farther than next door, but you had better get it going!" How true that is for each one of us. I have found that the Lord directs and steers a believer who is moving. If a believer is not moving, God cannot direct him. It is as we step out in faith and begin doing something For God, that He opens and closes doors for us.

> While starting a church in a small West Virginia town, I held my first few meetings in the town's municipal building. Before long we began to meet in a senior citizen's center. We continued later by meeting in a believer's home.
>
> While meeting in the home, proper foundations were laid and strong relationships were built. But I had to get started in the municipal building before God could direct us into the home. Move out and trust God to direct your paths.
>
> I would much rather try something and fail, than never try anything, and come to the end of my life and have nothing to show God. So what if you fail? At least you tried. "Where there are no oxen, the manger is empty, but from the strength of an ox comes an abundant harvest" (Prov. 14:4 NIV). Basically, this means if you never attempt to do any-thing for God, then there will be no messes, but if you are stepping out in service for God, you will make messes while also bringing in a harvest.
>
> So go, and if you head off in the wrong direction, trust the Lord to direct you back onto the right path!

8. *Cry out to God for His needed anointing!* He said, "You have not, because you ask not" (James 4:2). Begin to cry out diligently to the Lord for more of His power and anointing, all the while using what He has previously granted you. He will not give you more until you are using what you already have.

And when you ask, be sure you are asking out of correct motives, or you will be wasting your time. James 4:3 says, "Ye ask, and receive not, because ye ask amiss, that ye may consume it upon your lusts." Are you after the anointing so people will see how good and wonderful you are, or so that they will see how good and wonderful God's Son, Jesus, is?

Most importantly, ask in faith, "nothing doubting, for he that doubteth is like a wave of the sea driven with the wind and tossed. For let not that man think that he will receive anything from the Lord" (James 1:6–7). It is so necessary to have faith that God has heard, and has granted. Ask in faith, believing, and then go forth believing you have it.

As you minister, have faith in the anointing. That is, expect it to do the job it is supposed to do, as you do what you are supposed to do. Never go beyond the witness of your spirit in how far to step out with the anointing, but when you know it is present, just relax, knowing it will accomplish its task.

I once heard of a group of sincere, but misguided Christians who went to the dead body of a child two or three days after it had died. For several hours they commanded life to return to the body, while the director of the funeral home sympathetically allowed them to exercise their religious convictions. Though he was sympathetic, he was further convinced that serious Christian people are nothing more than wild-eyed fanatics who are totally out of touch with reality. The child's body remained lifeless and one by one the bereaved believers returned to their homes—crushed and embarrassed.

What was wrong? Does God not raise the dead today? Of course He does, and there are many medically affirmed and recorded incidents where this has happened. But unless God's Spirit specifically and powerfully witnesses to your spirit that this is what He wants to do at a given time, you are fooling yourself and wasting everyone's time by standing over a dead body and calling it back to life. Not only that, but you bring reproach on the Church of Jesus Christ.

The little group of believers learned a hard lesson that day. It would have been so much better had they been taught to never go beyond the strong witness of the Spirit in

126

their spirits concerning such matters as raising the dead. That is a miracle of such magnitude that unless the Spirit of God literally carries you through it, you make a fool of yourself by trying it without His very definite leading and support. I am sure that at least some of those precious believers felt they had the Holy Spirit's leading, but it is obvious they didn't. The child's body remained lifeless. I am convinced that had God truly spoken and instructed someone in that group of believers to raise that child from the dead, He would have also given them the "gift of faith" (1 Cor. 12:9) to help them receive the miracle.

On the other hand, when God does witness to your spirit that His anointing is present, and equal to the task at hand, it is so wonderful. You can just rest assured, knowing that the anointing will bring the desired result.

One day the Lord helped me to see this concept. It has released me from the desire to "feel" the anointing before I can "believe enough" to see its work. I know it is with me whether I feel it or not, because I do not depend on feelings. I have met the scriptural conditions; therefore, according to the Word of God, the anointing abides in and with me for the purpose of breaking yokes of bondage. And that's that!

Never did I have to rely on that fact as completely as I did when I was asked to preach at an open-air evangelistic meeting in Nakuru, Kenya, a few years ago. I had been teaching a Bible seminar to pastors and evangelists all day, and I was physically exhausted, and yet, I felt impressed of the Lord to accompany some African brothers to a large field in the middle of the city at nightfall for the purpose of preaching the gospel to a multitude of sinners. By the time we got to the field, hundreds of people had gathered to hear the Word of the Lord. Those precious folks were as hungry for the Word of God as any people I have ever seen. They were also riddled with sickness and disease. As I preached the gospel with a weary body, and a tired voice, I consciously exerted faith in the anointing I knew resided within me. It was not a strong and vibrant Chip Hill who destroyed Satan's yokes of bondage that night, it was the mighty anointing of God! Literally hundreds of people, of all

127

ages, were gloriously born-again, and also healed in their bodies before my very eyes. God was doing it. I did my part, He did His, and the outcome was victory!

My brother or sister, know that whatever God is calling you to do, His anointing for that job is available to you. Pursue it and win it! Do not be lazy where the anointing is concerned. Go after it in earnest, knowing that if you do not, you will never fulfill God's call on your life.

Before we close this chapter on the anointing of God, it would be good to look at one last passage from the Scriptures to help us see further the wondrous benefits of the anointing.

> I have found David my servant; with my holy oil have I anointed him: With whom my hand shall be established; mine arm also shall strengthen him. The enemy shall not exact upon him; nor the son of wickedness afflict him. I will beat down his foes before his face, and plague them that hate him. But my faithfulness and my mercy shall be with him: and in my name shall his horn be exalted. (Ps. 89:20–24)

This whole passage speaks of a spiritual anointing *and* its benefits. The servant David who is mentioned is King David of Israel, but it also looks forward to Jesus Christ who was prophesied to sit on the throne of David. This passage, in the truest sense, speaks of the anointing that would be upon Jesus. It is Christ Jesus' anointing, and it is *ours*!

In the days of Elijah and Elisha, Elisha received Elijah's mantle, and a double portion of his spirit (2 Kings 2:9–14). So today, we who wholeheartedly follow Jesus of Nazareth receive His mantle of power, and a strong dose of His mighty Spirit! His anointing is available for us if we will not turn back from following Him.

The benefits are wonderful.

His hand (signifying power) will be established with us.

His arm (signifying might) will strengthen us. Oh, how we need to have His arm in our goings forth!

"The enemy shall not exact from us [take anything from us by authority or force], or do us violence, or outwit us, or the wicked afflict and humble us." That is how it reads in the Amplified Bible.

God will beat our foes down before our faces, and plague those who hate us and burden themselves with us.

A number of years ago, a certain individual was spreading horrible and unfounded gossip about both me, and the spiritual work I was doing in my county. I could share with you the things he was saying, but it is almost too incredible for anyone to believe. Because he was ignorant, he knew not that the Scriptures warn, "Touch not mine anointed, and do my prophets no harm" (Ps. 105:15). Much damage was done to my reputation in the area because of the horrendous things he said. After a couple of years of this, the man literally lost every earthly thing he owned. His wife and kids left him. He lost hundreds of thousands of dollars in cattle futures. He lost his home, his farm, his vehicles and farm machinery. He lost a good-paying government job, and the retirement it would have paid him. And, worst of all, he lost a great deal of his sanity.

God says, "I'll plague those who hate you" (Ps. 89:23). I have seen this universal law of God go to work in other cases as well. You just cannot mess with God's anointed, and get away with it for very long. I believe that when Jesus knocked Saul from his horse on the road to Damascus, it was not just to get him saved, but to violently stop him from persecuting Christian people. Saul did the smart thing, and got saved. Had he not done so, he wouldn't have lasted very long. It is interesting to read the account. When Jesus confronted Saul He asked him why he was persecuting Him. Jesus took personally every bit of persecution that Saul had heaped upon the Christians. I believe the same holds true today.

Moving on in Psalm 89, we read that God's faithfulness and eternal mercy shall be with us wherever we are. Never is there a place, or a time, when God won't be with us. The Word also says that our "horns shall be exalted." Great power and prosperity shall be conferred upon us. When our horns are exalted, they are turned with the mouth upward so that we can catch the blessings pouring down from above.

Whoever you are, wherever you've been, if you will but

commit to follow the Son of God, Jesus Christ, with all of your heart, you will be anointed greatly for whatever He has called and commissioned you to do.

Know this: that all Christians should walk in a general anointing. In most cases it should be more than enough to put you over. But perhaps you are one of those who ministers with a special anointing. If so, please remember that it makes you no better than the next guy. It is only that God has called you to do a specific job, and you need more than the general anointing to do it accurately. Be diligent and see that special anointing increased.

Whatever the anointing you are blessed to walk in, carry it humbly. Thank God for it daily, and do those things that will insure its increasing effectiveness.

But the anointing which you have received of Him abides in you. (1 John 2:27)

Confession for the Child of God

Holy Father, I humbly thank you for the anointing which you have placed in me. As I search for you with all of my heart, soul, mind, and strength, through diligent study of your Word and your ways; through the privileged time of prayer; through regular fasting, and through practicing your presence day by day, I know it will increase ever so steadily.

I confess that the anointing abides within me, and according to this glorious fact, I will do exploits in your name.

The sick will be healed. Those vexed by demons will be liberated. The lost will be won into you Kingdom. Multitudes will go free from satanic bondage because of the anointing in and upon my life.

I have faith in you for this anointing. I shall go forth today and every day, rejoicing and trusting in the anointing to do its wonderful work.

Holy Lord, I thank you for the anointing in my life.

In Jesus' Name,
Amen.

130

10

The Violent and the Zealous

Hal Wallace is a man of God who will live forever in special places in God's Kingdom because he has given much of himself to seeing the captives set free. His own time and money have been offered freely in order to see people in bondage experience glorious liberation in Jesus' Name.

At the time of this writing Hal has been alive on this earth for eighty-three years. He is a young eighty-three (learned to water ski two years ago), and plans to be busy for God down here for a good while yet. All of us who know him believe he will. Hal's life has been an inspiration to multitudes of serious Christian people.

The thing about Hal that has inspired me, perhaps more than anything else, has been his violent nature (where spiritual things are concerned), and his ever-burning zeal for God.

Jesus said, "And from the days of John the baptist until now the kingdom of heaven suffers violence, and violent men take

131

it by force" (Matt. 11:12, NAS). That verse keynotes Hal's life, and it should in the lives of every elite commando warrior for God.

It is not speaking of a violence toward human beings, but a violence toward the work of hell. The enemy has stolen much ground from the kingdom of heaven here on the earth, and it's up to violent men and women of God to get it back! It will be by *force* that we will storm the gates of hell and take what is rightfully God's! It will involve the use of a violent faith, not a passive, nonchalant one. Norvel Hayes has said, "God doesn't bless nonchalant faith, but a ruthless faith." How true Brother Hayes's statement is. God is seeking to show himself strong in the lives of these violent men and women who are fed up with the works of hell and have resolved to destroy them wherever they are found!

A violent man or woman of God will learn about all that God has made available to them so as to be well-equipped when they enter into violent seasons of warfare. You show me a commando who has an unquenchable thirst for the Word of God, yea, an insatiable hunger for the things of God, and I'll show you a violent commando. Bible, books, tapes, prayer, enthusiastic praise, and the such, will be taking up most of this person's spare time. They forsake all in order to gain Christ! They are a violent soldier in God's victorious kingdom.

Standing alongside violence in importance in the life of the elite of God is zeal—pure unadulterated and uncomplicated jealousy over God and the things of God! In other words, godly zeal gets downright angry about things that are not pleasing to God and are dishonoring to Him.

Zeal motivated Elijah to mock four-hundred-and-fifty measly, down-in-the-mouth prophets of Baal!

Zeal motivated Phinehas to execute judgment on sin in the camp and stay a plague that had wiped out 24,000 of his people. God was so pleased over his act of zealousness that He commended and rewarded him publicly (Num. 25; Ps. 106:30).

Zeal quickened our excellent Lord to go into God's house with a scourge of cords and drive moneychangers and thieves from before its royal walls. As the text said, "Zeal for God's house consumed Him [ate Him up]" (John 2:13–17).

Paul commended the Corinthians for having a zeal to do justice to all, and to readily (not joyfully) mete out punishment to whom it was due (2 Cor. 7:11 TAB).

Zeal defined is a mixed passion, composed of grief and anger, fervent love and desire; for what a man loves earnestly, he is careful to see honored, and he is grieved when it is dishonored.

Zeal, in the biblical sense, has more to do with one's displeasure and resulting action over something displeasing and dishonoring to God than with someone's joyful excitement and enthusiasm for the things of God.

Have you ever gotten "hot under the collar" while watching the worldly talk-show host interview some liberal theologian about spiritual things? It seems they all answer the host's questions, not from the written Word of God, but from their own warped understanding of the Lord. How it tears you up! They condone homosexuality, support all the liberal special interest groups and are pro-choice abortionists 99 percent of the time. It makes me feel like putting my foot through the TV each time I hear them. They are not God's true representatives—they are counterfeits! Why don't the networks interview the real men and women of God? It makes me mad to see God lied about like that. That's the zeal of God working in me.

What drives Christians to picket abortion clinics? The zeal of God! For what makes God angry makes His people angry. And see how the pro-choicers hate the picketers. If there were no zeal, there would be no conflict.

Until the zeal of God once again becomes one of the prime motivations in the lives of Christian people, nothing more than what we have already seen will be accomplished for God's glory!

Our zeal will be a rascal to the world and a hypocritical church, but it will be the spark that ignites the greatest revival this world has ever seen. The zeal of God gets me to my feet as it burns in my bones.

If you want to be useful to an even greater degree than you've already been in God's Kingdom, begin to cry out to God for His much-needed zeal. Rise and shake yourself from the dust of indifference to what the devil has been doing around you, and with spiritual authority in hand, fire a shot that will be heard around the world. Drive your stake for the kingdom of Jesus and don't back down an inch. The greatest opportunities the Church has ever had lie before us. Victories that other Christians have only dreamed about are out there for you, but they will only be realized by the elite zealots of God! Determine to be among that number.

Genuine Godly Zeal

As prayer for the zeal of God is made for your life be sure your motives are in line with God's will. You know that it requires a certain amount of zeal and violence in order to experience God's power in manifestation. Yet, there may be a zeal and eagerness in the pursuit of the good things of God, when neither the end nor manner of doing it is good. For example, consider what the Word of God says of King Jehu of Israel. (see 2 Kings 9)

Jehu was anointed King of Israel that he might smite the evil house of Ahab, and avenge the blood of the prophets of God. Ahab, and particularly his wife Jezebel, were responsible for the undue slaughter of hundreds of God's anointed servants. God appointed the young zealot Jehu for the job of wiping out this evil blight, the house of Ahab.

Full of violence and the zeal of God, Jehu carried out his mission almost without flaw. As an elite Kingdom commando he went mercilessly through the entire ranks of Ahab's Kingdom, putting an end to Joram the son of Ahab, Ahaziah the king of Judah and a loyalist to Joram's evil reign, Jezebel, mother and true head of the entire evil kingdom, and the seventy tainted sons of Ahab who resided in Samaria. The Scriptures tell us that ". . . Jehu slew all that remained of the house of Ahab in Jezreel, and all his great men, and his kinsfolks, and his priests, until he left him none remaining" (2 Kings 10:11). Perhaps you are thinking, "Wow, what a wonderful man of God!" Wonderful as he may have been, there was one underlying, yet glaring problem involved in all he did. As eager in executing the commands of God as he was, we find that he did it to be seen and admired of men. In 2 Kings 10:16 we read of

Jehu inviting Jehonadab to "Come with me, and see my zeal for the Lord." This foundational, motivational character flaw (sin), which Jehu never dealt with was what eventually caused such degeneration in his commitment to the commands of God, that one of the final glimpses we get of him is that he ". . . took no heed to walk in the law of the Lord God of Israel with all his heart: for he departed not from the sins of Jeroboam, which made Israel to sin" (2 Kings 10:31). We must learn a lesson from Jehu's sad example.

While it is true that we all desperately need the zeal of God pounding in our hearts, we must never lose sight of the fact that it is all so that men might "see Jesus" and not look on us with undue praise and admiration. I must continually ask myself, "Chip, why do you do the things you do?" May I never say to another, "Come with me, and see my zeal for the Lord." But rather, "Come with me, and let us see Jesus."

So my brother and sister, desire the zeal of God, pray for it earnestly, move steadily into all that God has for you, knowing that the zeal of the Lord of hosts will perform great things (Isa. 9:7).

11

Go to Where They Are

I take delight in figuring out ways to plunder the prison houses of Satan on earth. There are countless ways in which a commando can launch excursions behind enemy lines where the prisoners of war are, and be successful on almost every mission. If we steep ourselves in fervent, effectual prayer, and discern the will and ways of God, He will lead and guide us into fertile territory. Before we launch out, we bind the strongman over the situation we are about to involve ourselves in, and by faith we lay hold on the special ability of God made available for us by the cross of Christ.

When we are planning an offensive, we need not broadcast our intentions for the world to know. Keep it secret between yourself and God and your fellow-team members. Employ only those men and women who are committed to excellence in their ministry as elite ones of God. This spiritual warfare is serious business, and eternal souls are at stake. There can be no "funny business."

I would like to share with you a few of the ways we go about setting the captives free from Satan's powers of death, sin, and sickness.

Individual Action

I challenge the members of our churches, "Ask God to develop in you the desire to be soul-winners." All of us are called by God to share His Son Jesus with those around us. It appalls me to see the number of Christians in this world who have no strong desire to see their fellow-human beings saved from the wrath to come. So many Christians are apathetic concerning the spiritual state of their families, friends, and neighbors. It was Jonathan Edwards who prayed, "Lord, stamp eternity on my eyeballs!" and he went on to win thousands to Jesus Christ. I would that every Christian begin to see every unsaved person in the light of eternal judgments. They shall all stand before the Judge of judges in the court of courts, and be condemned to eternity without God because they did not know Jesus. On that day they will be terrified because it will be a day when their entire pasts are exposed for all to see. As one man wrote, "God will take hold of history and empty it." All they have done that they've forgotten will be recalled—every idle word, every action—and God's mercy will not be there—only His wrath! We must warn them, because no one is good enough to escape "the white throne judgment" (Rev. 20:11–15). Only those who loved and obeyed Jesus in this life will be spared on that great day. We must warn them. But how?

Become a tract dispenser. In other words, be one of those commandos who keeps a good supply of gospel tracts in your shirt and coat pockets, in your glove compartment, and anywhere else that they may be easily reached in order to hand to the masses around you as God directs you. Besides handing them to brief acquaintances in public places, I delight in leaving them in public bathrooms, in motel dresser drawers, in phone booths, on store counters, or on restaurant tables (along with a good tip). During the summer, if I happen to walk past an automobile that has an open window, I toss a tract in on the seat, hoping that when the owner returns to the car, he will see

138

it and read it before throwing it away. In the back of all my tracts I have placed the sinner's prayer in simple words so that the person can read it and make genuine contact with Jesus Christ. Only eternity will tell just how many people have received Jesus through a cleverly placed gospel tract.

I also encourage the flocks in our various churches to write their own personal testimonies, and have them produced professionally in tract form. Many times a person will be sure to read your tract, because they are curious and will want to know all about you.

> My family and I were heading home from our summer vacation at Chincoteaque, Virginia last year when suddenly a hubcap sailed off of our car and went rolling out into the middle of a vast field where a man was mowing the grass with a large farm tractor. To our amazement the hubcap rolled right up to him and fell over. As I was turning the car around in order to go back and get the hubcap, the Lord told me to hand the man my personal testimony tract. It was clearly an appointment, ordained by God, for the benefit of that dear man. As I met him in the middle of the field I told him that what had happened was no mere coincidence, but that it was ordained by God so that I might share the love of Jesus with him. The man was speechless. I talked with him only briefly, telling him of Jesus' great love for him, and as I handed my personal testimony tract to him he received it as though it was fragile china. As we went our separate ways— he back to his work and my family and me back down the highway, my wife, Darlene, could see him riding off on his tractor earnestly pouring over the words of my tract.
>
> So often I have seen the personal testimony tract used as an invaluable tool for effective evangelism. Don't leave home without it.

I have written many different tracts on different topics which I use to hand to specific people at specific times. For instance, I have a tract entitled "Healing," and another one entitled, "God's Provision of Healing" which I hand to people who are experiencing sickness and disease. These go like hot cakes in the hospitals. I have another tract entitled, "The Occult—It May Be the Cause of Your Problems," and one called "Curses," that I slip into the "trash" newspapers lining the checkout counters in the grocery stores. Also, with stealth, I place these two titles in the books on witchcraft and astrology that can be found in most of the bookstores down at the mall. While there, I slip (in commando fashion, of course) over to the section with all the weight-lifting and body-building books. Inside of these I place my tract, "The Fraility of Physical Life." I have written many other tracts that suit different occasions, because I believe in being well-equipped for kingdom service. Who knows but that my tract might be just what's needed to save a soul from hell.

As an individual I also look for God-ordained opportunities to share Jesus with other individuals as God brings us together. Even if it is just for a moment I try to speak a word in season what may open up the conversation for Jesus. If it doesn't happen, I can at least give them my personal-testimony tract, and rejoice in the fact that our brief encounter on the journey of life wasn't wasted. I believe in seizing every opportunity to witness for Christ. More than one salesman has left my home as a new-born Christian as a result of my seizing that unique opportunity. They came to sell something to me, only to be given the love of Jesus. Don't be so quick to turn everyone away from your door. I have found most door-to-door salesmen to be empty, hurting, and crying out for acceptance. Do you think they like having doors closed in their faces? You don't have to buy their products, but you do have to tell them about Jesus.

The hospitals, the prisons, or the houses down at the city dump; regardless of what part of the country they are found in, there are broken lives there that must be given the opportunity to receive the healing Christ. Don't wait for a convenient time to go to them, but make certain times to go. As I stated in an earlier chapter, "Good intentions don't win wars." Get yourself a calandar, and schedule your rescue mission; that is the only way you'll utilize time in this life for this important business of salvaging human lives.

Team Action

Just as the crack Israeli commandos swept into Uganda and set their countrymen free from Idi Amin's Entebbe Airport turned prison, we like to sweep, with a team of people, into the hospitals of our land and liberate the hostages held there.

An elite group of us, trained in the skills of soul-winning, launch out from our church in the western mountains of Virginia, and drive one hundred or so miles to the University of Virginia Hospital in Charlottesville. Armed with pockets full of tracts of all descriptions, we split up in teams of two, or we go individually, and work the floors of this massive hospital. What we face are corridors and corridors of hurting and frightened people. There is the little black woman in the wheelchair out in the hall—all alone, and needing some good news. Down in the lobby, a worried mother waits for the doctor's report concerning her baby. Perhaps for the first time in her life she is ready to hear about a compassionate Savior who heals little babies.

In large hospitals, each floor usually has a big room with sofas and TV sets where patients who are not too sick can go to while away a few hours before returning to their hospital rooms. We have found these ambulatory patients to be very receptive to our message of love and healing.

I like to slip down the hall, from room to room, looking for the invalids with no guests, no family, and no friends by their sides. The realization that a total stranger would bother to come to them and offer a simple prayer, is usually more than they can take. They'll break down and cry as their hearts soften and become receptive for the impartation of divine life from above.

When we first arrive in the main lobby of the University Hospital, we synchronize our watches. We will all get together every couple of hours, if at all possible, in order to encourage one another, witness to a victory, and plan our strategy for the next excursion. We have found this strategy to be very successful. Let me show you how.

Suppose I meet a patient whose situation is such that the

gifting on one of my fellow-commandos is better suited to winning the patient, or simply gaining a certain victory for the patient. When we meet in the lobby the next time, I can secure the aid of the special commando, and together we can go to the needy patient.

Another benefit of coming together at certain times during the day is that this will enable each one of us to tap into the corporate counsel of the entire group. Proverbs 24:6 says, "By wise counsel thou shalt make war." Remember, in the hospital we are to be making war on the works of hell, and loving the captives into the Kingdom of God.

I believe you can see the limitless possibilities for ministry in this type of hospital strategy.

One last thing on hospital ministry. It is of utmost importance that each commando behave himself decently and orderly while working the various floors of the hospital. Never place yourself between a nurse or a doctor and the patient. Stringently obey the hospital's visiting hours. (Pastors will be an exception). It is also important that each member of the team dress nicely when visiting the hospital; smell nice, look nice, act nice—be rude and nasty only to the demon spirits you may come against. Maintain a low volume of voice, unless the patient is hard of hearing, so as not to disturb the other patients in the room or on the ward. Remember, you want to be welcomed back, and not rejected by the hospital authorities.

Other possibilities for teams of commando warriors are found in the many nursing homes or convalescent centers throughout our land. There is always a person waiting inside who is ready to hear what you have to offer.

Taking teams to work the shopping malls is a good way to reach out to the lost of humanity. Sit on a bench next to a total stranger and strike up a friendly conversation; see where you can take it, and offer to them your personal-testimony tract. The possibilities are tremendous.

Grocery stores are good places to meet the public, maybe not as a large team, but as an individual, or a twosome.

City parks, public pools, etc., provide similar opportunities.

Be creative and dare to step out by scheduling your excursion into the areas where fellow-men sit enslaved.

Another way to evangelize is to contact the people in your neighborhood socially. By this I mean to look for things you have in common with them, and begin to get together with them on a fairly regular basis. So long as you don't compromise your integrity and Christian witness, you are okay. We found a family down the road from us who loved to watch John Wayne westerns, so we began to have them over to our house for supper and a John Wayne VCR movie about once a month. We developed a strong friendship with them and in time we were able to share Jesus effectively. It is all right to do "secular" things with the unbelievers around you. Remember, Jesus was a friend of sinners.

12

What Lies Ahead for the Elite of God?

The chapter title is a loaded question and I could devote a series of books to its answer. Instead, I'll briefly discuss a few things that come to mind, and what God has been showing me for quite some time.

First of all, I see an increase of demonic activity coming our way. The hosts of Satan's kingdom have much to fear where we are concerned, and they will be giving special assignment to certain demons who will be sent to "trip up," as it were, those of us who are militant commando warriors for God.

What are some of the ways in which they will attack?

There will be a bombardment of sexual temptation. This has proven, and will continue to prove to be a very successful way in which Satan knocks the commando out of the way. I could name many men of God from the last decade who have made shipwreck of their ministries because they gave over to this time-proven tactic of the enemy. The Delilah spirit, one of seduction, is very active against men in the ministry today. Ministers who once had tremendous influence in the Body of Christ, have succumbed to the "seductive spirits" Satan has unleashed in these final days of the twentieth century (2 Tim. 3:13).

This may be shocking to you, yet I consider it a conservative percentage—60 percent of today's young ladies are pawns in the hands of a seductive spirit. That's a conservative estimate. You see it in the way they conduct themselves, the way they dress, the way they walk and talk, and by the crowds they run with. Is it any wonder that most of America's young men are puddy in the hands of demons of lust and promiscuous sex? I can recognize a seductive spirit in a woman a mile away. That demon of seduction is bred into them and pounded into them from birth by worldly parents and the ungodly society in which we live. The music many listen to feeds this lust within them. Movies and TV shows pound it into us, and the magazines on the magazine racks make lust appear decent. Girls learn early what guys like and by the time they are young adults, they are pros at exploiting the uncontrolled passions in men. Lust reigns supreme in our culture.

The tragedy is that many Christian boys and men are falling victim to these seductive spirits. I know of multitudes of young, would-be soldiers of God who have fallen prey to these seductive forces—found many times in Christian women. You would be appalled at the incredible number of Christian young men, or older men, married and unmarried, who daily fall to the lusts of their flesh in the area of sex.

Pornography has often been the first step of many that have spiraled down to ruin in the lives of countless Christian men. Masturbation has become a way of life to many who say they have called on the name of the Lord to be saved. Fornicators, adulterers, homosexuals, child abusers, masturbators—all can be found through most segments of professing Christendom.

The Word of God reveals that a time is coming when "The sinners in Zion [the Church] will be afraid; and that fearfulness will surprise the hypocrites" (Isa. 33:14, paraphrase mine).

People who think they are getting by with sexual sin in their lives should not be deceived. A time of great exposure is nigh at hand, if they fail to repent and turn from their wickedness. God's *now* word to you, if you're guilty of sexual sin, is, "Forsake your wicked way, and forsake your unrighteous thoughts; and return to me, and I will have mercy on you, and I will abundantly pardon" (Isa. 55:7, paraphrase mine).

Jesus said (in Matthew 13:41), that He will one day "send forth His angels, and they shall gather *out of His kingdom* all things that offend, and them which do iniquity; and shall cast them into a furnace of fire."

The time has come for all who claim to be Christian to clean up their acts. Men, stop entertaining the seductive spirits of pornography—whether it be hard-core, or the lingerie section of the department store catalogue. Wives, keep those catalogues put away if your man has had problems with lust in the past. He has enough pressure from Satan without you lending a helping hand. Do not be so naive as to think he cannot be affected.

I am also appalled at the increasing number of Christian girls who are dressing more seductively these days. At a picnic recently, my wife and I were shocked to witness a young "sister in the Lord" who was gathering much lustful attention from her "brothers in Christ" by what she was (should I say-*wasn't*) wearing. She was clad with nothing but a skimpy halter-top, and the shortest, little pair of shorts I've seen in a long time. What's even worse is that she was only fifteen years old and a professing Christian. This was not merely a once-in-a-while occurrence—it happens all the time in Christian circles, and it ought not to be. No sister, however old she may be, has the right to put an "occasion for stumbling" in a brother's path. That girl's mom, and particularly her dad, should have never allowed her to leave her bedroom in that seductive fashion.

Sexual Sin Kills!

The horror of sexual sin is that it kills. All manner of spiritual, soulish and physical problems will be its deadly result. One may seem to get by with it for a season, but stand assured, sexual sin will find you out! Is it any wonder that Paul exhorted young Timothy to "Flee youthful lusts" (2 Tim. 2:22)? He went on to say that if you do not, you can come to the time when you are taken captive of Satan at his will!

Paul also exhorted the Christian church at Corinth to "Flee fornication." He said that "every sin that a man does is without the body; but he who commits fornication sins against his own body" (1 Cor. 6:18). A homosexual AIDS victim can testify to that! A prostitute riddled with gonorrhea can say "amen" to that!

Did you know that the Word of God says that lust is "a fire that consumes to destruction, and would root out all your increase" (Job 31:12)? All that God has done for you can be burned up or rooted out because of your lust. Come on, would-be commando warrior for Jesus, get control of your passions and reign in life by your Lord Jesus Christ! If you don't, you will suffer much loss—mark my words!

If you are one who has been enslaved by the clever spirit of seduction; if you are one who is bound by some ungodly sexual habit; if you have cried out to God for freedom from it, and freedom has not come—I'll tell you what to do.

If you are a man, confide in a strong Christian brother. Appeal to him for prayer support, his availability to you in your times of testing, and for encouragement should you fall. Go to a pastor, an elder, a home group leader, a good, strong Christian brother, etc. Whatever you do, don't try to whip the problem alone, especially if it has held you in its power for a considerable amount of time.

Sister, perhaps you are under the control of a seductive spirit. Does the way in which you dress, walk, or perhaps hug your brother cause him to stumble? And maybe the seductive spirits of the world are hanging you up. Are you in bondage to a daytime soap opera? The adultery and sexual misconduct on these sour offerings from Hollywood are promoted as being "not that bad." Maybe you live in a romantic fantasy world and you need to get back to reality. Confide in a strong Christian sister. Get free!

As far as teenagers are concerned, I feel sorry for them. Especially the boys. It is tough to stay a chaste Christian male, for everywhere a young man turns, the world, with it's loose morals, is slamming temptation after temptation at them. But I can say from experience that there is victory in Jesus. He has not left us comfortless and feeble. He has given us the grace whereby we can overcome—every time! Stand up in Jesus' name and say "No!" to sin. You can do it if you want to bad enough.

You know, it's really a cop-out to blame one's declining spirituality on the rampant, sensual temptations in the world. It is wrong to blame only the setting in which one finds himself. Why? Because if one will continue to do those things which are necessary for spiritual life and vitality, he will "abound" spiritually in spite of all the vice and corruption around him. In the midst of a hell of sensuality and temptation, if you continue to feed on fresh manna from heaven (God's Word) daily, and drink the water from the Rock (Jesus), on a continuous basis—you'll live and abound. So let's not merely blame settings for the downfall of Christian people. Had they continued in His Word, they would have been and remained free (John 8:32). I think we can all say "Amen" to that, and that from personal experience. How strong are you now? Are you doing those things necessary for spiritual growth? You are to rule and reign in life wherever you are and whenever you are.

Don't think you are getting away with anything. "Because sentence against an evil work is not executed swiftly" the Bible says, "the heart of the sons of men is fully set in them to do evil" (Eccles. 8:11). But "be not deceived, God is not mocked; whatsoever a man soweth, that shall he also reap" (Gal. 6:7). If you continue to sow the wind, you shall "reap the whirlwind" (Hos. 8:7). "For he that sows to his flesh shall of the flesh reap corruption" (Gal. 6:8a). Be a forewarned, forearmed Christian.

Jesus was a radical teacher. He taught us how to overcome sin in our lives. Today He tells us to "Mortify sin in our members" (Col. 3:5), telling us that if something is an offense to us, "cut it off" (Matt. 5:29–30)! If the television is giving you a hard time, with its gorgeous girls "gracing" its screen, get rid

149

of the thing! Better for the TV to go the way of the garbage heap, than you. Deal ruthlessly with the things Satan is using to topple you, and allow him no headway. Job made a "covenant with his eyes" saying, "how then could I gaze at a virgin" (Job 31:1 NAS). Make a covenant with your eyes that you will only look where God wants you to look. Reign in life by Jesus Christ!

Another pressure that lies ahead for the elite of God is persecution which will be designed to shut your mouth. The demon spirit, "the fear of man," is being unleashed against all true ministers of the gospel. Verbal attacks, such that you have not dreamed of, will be launched in your direction as you go about to set the captives free. Satan does not take joyfully the spoiling of his kingdom. He will set tongues wagging against you. People in high places will become a threat to you. The enemy will seek to make you worry about what people think. He wants you to veer away from declaring the whole counsel of God to this perverse and lost generation. He will use social pressure, political pressure, denominational pressure, and financial pressure in order to silence you.

Stand strong. Jesus said, "What I tell you in secret, shout from the housetops!" (Matt. 10:27, paraphrased). Paul exhorted us to, "Preach the Word; be instant in season, out of season" (2 Tim. 4:2a). Do not be afraid of what man may say, or think, or do. God's word to you is, "Be not afraid of their faces; for I am with thee to deliver thee" (Jer. 1:8). He further says, "Gird up your loins and arise, and speak unto them all that I command thee; be not dismayed at their faces, lest I confound thee before them" (Jer. 1:17). "Like an adamant [a very hard stone] have I made thy forehead: fear them not, neither be dismayed at their looks, though they be a rebellious house [and will likely disagree wholeheartedly with you]" (Ezek. 3:9, paraphrase mine).

Hey, pastor, what will happen if you offend your rich members? Young man, what will happen if your declaration of the Word offends your mom, your dad, or a long-time friend? Don't worry about it if you know God has told you to declare it. Trust Him to bring them around to your point of view. Much of what commandos are called on to say and to do will be "hard sayings" in the ears of many.

> I have a friend who pastors a church nearby. There came a day when he stood fearlessly to proclaim a certain powerful word he felt was from the heart of God. The nature of the word was such that it challenged his parishioners to live lives of holiness and not to compromise in the community. His message maddened certain members and they promptly aired their disapproval to the district superintendent of his denomination.
>
> An ultimatum came forth promptly to my young pastor friend: "Either shape up or ship out!" He was warned not to rock the boat and not to offend the members of his church.
>
> It saddens me to have to report that today he is doing anything he has to in order to win the approval of both his superiors and his parishioners. If he isn't careful, he will lose his job, and so he compromises before the wicked. The Scriptures say he is as: "A muddied fountain and a polluted spring" who "yields, falls down, and compromises his integrity before the wicked" (Prov. 25:26 TAB). Oh, the sin of compromise!

Are you a called man or a hireling? A hireling flees when he sees trouble coming. A called man won't run from anything! A called man says and does whether he gets paid or not; whether it is accepted or not. Are you called into elite kingdom service?

I see persecution coming against true Christians. Another reason is because the wealth of the world is coming to us. We are going to be the most influential people on the face of the earth before it's all over with. The Word of God testifies to this very fact. (See Prov. 13:22; Ps. 111:6; Eccles. 2:26; Job 27:16–17; Prov. 28:8; Hag. 2:7).

Psalms 2 speaks of a time coming when "the heathen will rage, . . . and the kings of the earth will set themselves, and the rulers will take counsel together, against the Lord, and against his anointed [ones] saying, "Let us break their bands asunder and cast away their cords from us (Ps. 2:1–3). If the leaders of nations ever get together about anything else, I don't know. But the Word says they will come together in order to see the people of God destroyed. We are destined to become a very influential people in the earth. As we operate the laws of the kingdom, such as the law of reciprocity, we will become the great finance handlers of all time. The greed of ungodly men won't tolerate that, so they will declare war on Christians.

Can it happen? Read your Bible. It has happened down through the centuries. Will we be defeated? No, thank God, "He that sits in the heavens shall have them in derision" (Ps. 2:4). If God be for us, who can successfully be our enemies? Satan cannot, neither can mere pawns in his hands. So look ahead, commando. Days of great financial inversion are at hand. We are destined to secure more than enough capital, and this will help us to proclaim the gospel to the entire world, and then shall the end come (Matt. 24:14).

Another thing that lies ahead for the elite of God, which is not of a positive nature, is increased occult and cult activity. People all over the world have a fascination with the supernatural, and this is leading multitudes into bondage and demonic vexation.

There are only two sources of hidden information and help in the world. Both are supernatural and cannot be obtained by natural means. One source is the One, true God—the God of Abraham, Isaac, and Jacob, and His channel of blessing is Jesus Christ. Philippians 4:19 reveals, "But my God shall supply all your need—by Jesus Christ." Jesus Christ of Nazareth is the only way by which God reaches mankind, and He is the only way by which mankind can reach God (John 14:6; 1 Tim. 2:5).

The other source of hidden knowledge and "help" is Satan, and his kingdom of darkness. The Word of God tells us that he deceives, seduces, and works lying wonders.

Hidden information can be had through both of these sources, but to go to Satan is to call upon another god, which is clearly condemned by the Bible. "You shall have no other gods before Me" (Exod. 20:3).

Going to the kingdom of darkness for any help or information is what the occult is all about. To seek anything from Satan's kingdom is to break faith with God and commit spiritual adultery! To do so, even innocently, is to invoke a curse. The Bible says, "Their sorrows shall be multiplied that hasten after another god" (Ps. 16:4).

By seeking another god (a demon) through occult involvement, one automatically opens the door of his life for a curse to waltz right in. Dabbling in the occult gives Satan and his emissaries a legal right to come into one's life to vex, harrass, and oppress him.

The same holds true for anyone, regardless of how innocent or sincere, who seeks to know or serve God through any of the many cults that are in the earth today.

Some of these are Mormonism, Bahaism, Hinduism, Buddhism, Mohammedanism, Jehovah's Witnesses, the Moonies, Masonic Lodges and Eastern Star. (It doesn't matter what businessmen or high-society people are in them).

> The acid test which proves the error of these and many other religions or "fraternities" (and many are accepted as Christian), is what place they readily give to Jesus. Unless Jesus Christ is central, and unless He has the preeminence in everything the organization is and seeks to do, no matter how noble and good, it is not Christian, and according to Romans 3:10–12, is a dead work, unacceptable to God the Father who made the supreme sacrifice in giving up His only begotten Son to die on the cross for all mankind. Unless a "religion continually points man to Christ, and Christ alone, it is not serving His purpose in the earth. That is why we must reject the aforementioned religious organizations or so-called fraternities. Jesus Christ of Nazareth is not their only Lord!

Regardless of the extent of one's involvement, the activity of demon spirits has been welcomed in, a curse is operating, and only the power of Jesus Christ can totally free the person involved.

As commando warriors, we must know how to set people free from the various curses that may be operating in their lives. If a curse is present, prayer will not be sufficient many times. The minister with the Word and power of God must be able to detect the presence of a curse, and to break its hold over the victim.

Some of the signs of a curse are:

Mental or emotional breakdowns in the life of the victim. Spiritual oppressions and obsessions will show up if the person has delved into the occult or a cult. There will generally be a breakdown in the marriage covenant if one or both of the partners have been involved in the occult. There will be family alienation, bad relationships between the family members, unruly and disobedient children (Deut. 28:41). Cursed people will experience frequent or prolonged seasons of depression or gloom; indifference; irresponsibility; unpredictable behavior; delusions; uncontrollable passions and appetites; sexual perversions; enslavement to drugs, alcohol, and tobacco; tormenting fears; suicidal thoughts and tendencies; reccuring nightmares; compulsive feelings of hate, jealousy, and violence; seeing apparitions; hearing voices; poltergeist phenomena; miscarriages and related female problems; deformed children; indifference to spiritual things—the Bible and praying; chronic doubts and difficulty exercising faith; abnormal talkativeness and loudness; unkempt appearance; abnormal eyes—glazed, sullen, perverse or blank; abnormal facial countenances; continual financial difficulties; a proneness to accidents, either in one person's life or the lives of family members; repeated and chronic sickness, especially those which never get clearly diagnosed. And the list can go on.

As a deliverance minister, the elite person of God must know that the basic provision of God for the release from all curses is the atonement of Jesus Christ on the cross. Galatians 3:13 says that Jesus "redeemed us from the curse of the law." He took upon himself the entire evil inheritance due to us because of our sin. On the cross He not only suffered our punishment, but He exhausted the curse.

As God's commando encounters someone who is suffering under the weight of a curse, and the person indicates that he wants help, the minister must first be absolutely positive that

154

the person is saved or born again by the blood, Spirit, and Word of Jesus. If they are not, then by all means introduce them to Jesus and lead them through the sinner's prayer.

Secondly, by the help of the Holy Spirit, have them recall every form of the occult and/or cults they have ever been involved with, and renounce them in Jesus' Name. Ask the Holy Spirit to help them recall these various practices and beliefs. Also, be open for the gift of "a word of knowledge" to be operative in your life (1 Cor. 12:8).

Third, make sure that the victim forgives from his heart all people who have in any way wronged him. Jesus taught that the unforgiveness of a man's heart can open him up to demonic torment in his life (Matt. 18:34). Remember to show them that the initial act of forgiving someone is done by an act of their wills, not so much because they *feel* like the person is forgiven. We forgive because we *choose to forgive*. The Bible teaches that forgiveness, like love, is a gift. If it is a free gift, then how can the one you choose to forgive earn it? If they could earn it, then it would no longer be a free gift. Help them to see this.

Fourth, take them through the actual ministry of deliverance. Teach them to cooperate with you, to be humble, and to exercise faith toward God that He will see to it that nothing is left concealed.

Use the power and authority of the Name of Jesus Christ, the blood of the Lamb, the Word of God, and the Spirit of God within you. You have been given authority over all devils (Luke 9:1). If you do not use that authority in an aggressive manner, you will not be setting many free from the power of curses.

Fifth, stress to the person whom you have ministered to the importance of continuing in the Word (John 8:31–32), getting into and staying in fellowship with strong believers, and being maintained full of the Holy Spirit. If they are not baptized with the Holy Spirit, then see to it that they are!

All of these things are very important. The Bible teaches that if a demon spirit is forced to leave a man, it may not be long before he returns and seeks to gain entrance back into the man. If he can do so he may take other demons more vile than himself with him and the man will be worse off in this latter state than he was in the beginning.

A man came to me a few years ago seeking deliverance. For years he had been a member of a motorcycle gang that was known for its riotous activities. While with them he had indulged in sexual orgies, taken many kinds of drugs, and delved deeply into various forms of the occult. Needless to say, he was terribly demonically oppressed. He claimed to know Jesus, saying he had prayed to receive Him a couple of years before. My wife and I arranged to take him to Hal and Helen Wallace in Staunton, Virginia, for deliverance. His case was such that we wanted their expertise involved in securing his deliverance. Hal and Helen were veterans in the ministry of deliverance with many years of experience to their credit.

Deliverance took about four hours with the man and he was visibly and gloriously set free. Demons came out of him, crying and screaming and soundly fleeing. He was a changed man.

We stressed to him the responsibilities he now had in order to maintain his freedom—Bible reading and study, prayer, ample fellowship with other Christians, etc. We cautioned him not to go back and get involved with his old crowd. We did all we could do to insure his growth in the Lord. But he did not take heed to our instructions. Before long he was back with the same old crowd of drinking buddies and was no longer seen in fellowship with believers. When his demons returned they found him waiting. They simply reentered him, taking many more demons with them. His last state is today far worse than his former state. Since his deliverance he has been convicted of a murder that he admits to and is accused by many of being the felon in another murder.

He is facing life in prison and if he were to be given his freedom, there are those friends and relatives of the man or men that he killed that might eagerly gun him down. He is a hated man and one who is finding no support. All because he failed to take the Word of God as seriously as he should have.

The importance of helping the victim of demonic oppression see his responsibility of staying in the Word of God and prayer, and in fellowship is seen so clearly in the example I just gave. There is a price to be paid in order to remain free. If we fail to stress this to them, we do them an injustice by freeing them from what demons they do have, and we may in fact make matters worse.

The frontal attack of Satan by means of the occult is on an upswing in this day and hour. The Word of God reveals that it will only get worse, and that perilous times are going to abound.

As people seek the supernatural in ways other than Jesus Christ, they will be enslaved. Only those equipped with the weaponry of God will be able to help them.

The generation of kids around us are enslaved by rock music which is clearly an occult involvement. "Slop" magazines are displayed at every checkout counter, in every supermarket in the country. Gracing their abominable covers are headlines similar to this: "Madame Dingbat Gives Her Twenty-One Predictions for *Your* Life." Gullible homemakers by the thousands buy and read these spewed-out-of-hell offerings and find that certain segments of their lives begin to fall apart—and they don't know why.

Elite warrior for God, prepare yourself to counter this work of hell. Arm yourself for the fray at hand, and God will project you into the arena of war. Countless thousands await you. I believe you will answer the call.

What good lies ahead for us? Untold opportunities! If you will but "Lift up your eyes, and look on the fields" (John 4:35), you'll see the world is white, ripe, and ready to be harvested. If you'll go forth to reap, you'll be gathering fruit unto eternal life.

As we prepare ourselves for God's service, He promises to open up doors of opportunity to us that will be truly remarkable. As you walk in God, allowing your hands to be *His* hands, your voice to be *His* voice, your money to be *His* money, you will personally witness the release of countless hostages out of Satan's kingdom. People will literally seek you out, because they know you have the "words of truth" that

157

can set them free (Prov. 22:17–21). They'll grab handfuls of your clothing, saying, "We will go with you, for we see that God is with you" (Zech. 8:23, paraphrase mine).

You may ask, "How can this be?" Just watch and see the effect of God on the hearts of multitudes in the coming days. People laid the sick in the streets, hoping that Peter's shadow would fall upon them. They took handkerchiefs from Paul's body so that demons would leave those on whom the handkerchiefs were laid. The crowds thronged, and pressed in upon Jesus wherever He went. When faith pioneer Smith Wigglesworth took a train to another town, mobs awaited him, seeking his healing touch. Those days will return again. The only difference will be that it will not be an occassional Wigglesworth here, or a Peter there; there will be literally thousands of committed commando warriors going about the entire earth, doing the works of Jesus; achieving the exploits of God (Dan. 11:32b).

The POW's await you, my brother and sister. The captives' cries are mounting up to heaven. God is preparing an army, and He desires your participation. Are you readying yourself? Can we count on your participation?

Judge yourself for character. Make sure your motives are correct. If they are, you'll have no trouble serving on another man's team. If they're wrong, submission will tear you up. Remember, if you humble yourself, God will exalt you in due time. Leave that with Him and resist the temptation to exalt yourself. The way up is down. Just be faithful where you are and watch God move in your behalf when He is ready. Don't force His hand, because this will bring shame and destruction.

Study to show yourself approved and ready. Establish yourself, knowing who you are in Jesus Christ, and Who He is in you. Build a firm and proper foundation for ministry.

Allow God to sock you into a local church that is going somewhere. Get linked up with a people who have vision. Become a follower of those who, through faith and patience, are inheriting the promises (Heb. 6:12).

Endure hardness of training as a good soldier of Jesus Christ. Do not expect a picnic each day of your life. It is through much tribulation that we enter the kingdom. Stay on your toes, because your adversary, the devil, goes about as a roaring lion, seeking whom he may devour. "Watch ye therefore, and pray always, that ye may be accounted worthy to escape all these things that shall come to pass, and to stand before the Son of man (Luke 21:36).

13

Final Words

In closing this book, I would like to exhort you with a word that has meant as much to me perhaps as any I have heard to date. It goes something like this:

If you would do the *best* with your life, find out what God is doing in your generation, and throw yourself unreservedly into the midst of it.

My brother or sister, if you will but make that little line of exhortation your mandate for life, you will go far in this kingdom's service.

As I stated at the outset of this book, you have as much as God has to say concerning your accomplishments in His Kingdom on earth.

Paul said, "In a great house there are not only vessels of gold and of silver, but also of wood and of earth; and some to honor, and some to dishonor." He went on to say, "If a man would purge himself" [from the things of the world; from the foreign matter that seeks to cling to him; from the sin which does so easily beset him; and from anything that would serve as a hindrance to his fulfilling his destiny in God] then, that man would be "a vessel unto honor, sanctified, and fit to be used by the Master, and prepared for every good work" (2 Tim. 2:20–21).

In a great house of visible Christendom, there are all kinds. God seeks those who have "counted the cost," committed themselves totally to His loving Lordship, and have received a baptism of His love, boldness, and power, to go and set this world free from it's froward way.

Above all—be real!

As you grow in the things He teaches you, and as you discover many other ways in which to be of service to Him, be sure that the impressions you set forth are genuine. Hold to an unfeigned maturity. If you are not fifty years old in the faith don't try to deceive people into thinking you are. It will not work! Paul addresses this in his first epistle to young Timothy:

> But the goal of our instruction is love, out of a pure heart and a good conscience and a sincere faith. (1 Tim. 1:5).

A sincere or unfeigned faith is what God is after in His people. Too many times we see young Christians going about talking as though they are forty years old in the Lord. They have listened to all the latest teaching tapes, have read all the best-selling Christian books, and watch the "700 Club" every day. With all these precious tools for growth it is easy to be lulled into thinking, "I've arrived, brother!" But the truth is that you really are not who you think you are until you are that person under pressure. Possessions you may think are yours really aren't unless you have and hold them when the storms hit.

I have seen Christians sit at fellowship meals and banter the verses of victory back and forth like they are old warhorses. After all, they've got the right words too! But you ought to see them when the storm hits. Whew! They squall like mashed cats. You see, you can sometimes fool men with your jargon, but you will not fool the devil, and you certainly cannot fool God. So you might as well be real, genuine, transparent. Is what you banter back and forth with your brothers and sisters just words or is it revelation knowledge borne deep in your heart, and a well-laid foundation? If it is reality in your life, when the floods come, you will stand in Jesus' Name!

God's purpose for you right now is that you throw off all masks and be *real* before your brothers and sisters in Christ. Be a genuine man or woman of God and insist that others be genuine in front of you. This is the only way we will be able to spot each other's weaknesses early and really be of help to one another. If I am always trying to fool you into thinking I am someone I am not, we will be of no real benefit to one another. Ask yourself this question: "Just who am I trying to impress anyway?" If you find you've been missing it here, get it right and start immediately to be genuine in front of all.

You Are a Commando for God

This book, though not exhaustive, has helped you to grasp a little more of the vision God is giving to the Body of Christ in this hour of world history. As you commit your life and energies to serving His purposes in your lifetime He will empower and embolden you to do much in this world for His eternal glory.

When you come to the end of the race that is now set before you, and when, through faithfulness and endurance, you finish your course, you shall be forever rewarded with the most precious words of your Savior, Lord, and Redeemer, *"Well done, good and faithful servant; enter thou into the everlasting joy of the Lord."*

RISE UP, O MAN OF GOD. HAVE DONE WITH LESSER THINGS.
GIVE HEART, AND SOUL, AND MIND, AND STRENGTH,
TO SERVE THE KING OF KINGS . . .
TO SERVE THE KING OF KINGS.